BATH

[*Design Guide*]

Better Homes and Gardens® Bath Design Guide
Contributing Editor/Writer: Lexicon Consulting, Inc.
Associate Design Director: Todd Emerson Hanson
Contributing Graphic Designer: Matthew Eberhart, Evil Eye Design, Inc.
Copy Chief: Terri Fredrickson
Copy Editor: Kevin Cox
Publishing Operations Manager: Karen Schirm
Senior Editor, Asset & Information Management: Phillip Morgan
Edit and Design Production Coordinator: Mary Lee Gavin
Editorial Assistant: Kaye Chabot
Book Production Managers: Pam Kvitne, Marjorie J. Schenkelberg,
    Mark Weaver
Imaging Center Operator: Scott A. La Mar
Contributing Copy Editor: Kim Catanzarite
Contributing Proofreaders: Judy Arginteanu, Kristi Berg, Nancy Ruhling
Contributing Indexer: Sharon Duffy

Meredith® Books
Editor in Chief: Gregory H. Kayko
Executive Director, Design: Matt Strelecki
Managing Editor: Amy Tincher-Durik
Executive Editor: Benjamin W. Allen
Senior Editor/Group Manager: Vicki Leigh Ingham
Senior Associate Design Director: Ken Carlson
Marketing Product Manager: Brent Wiersma

Executive Director, Marketing: Kevin Kacere
Executive Director, Sales: Ken Zagor
Director, Operations: George A. Susral
Director, Production: Douglas M. Johnston
Director, Marketing & Publicity: Amy Nichols
Business Director: Jim Leonard

Senior Vice President: Karla Jeffries
Vice President and General Manager: Douglas J. Guendel

Better Homes and Gardens® **Magazine**
Editor in Chief: Gayle Goodson Butler
Deputy Editor, Home Design: Oma Blaise Ford

Meredith Publishing Group
President: Jack Griffin
Executive Vice President: Doug Olson

Meredith Corporation
Chairman of the Board: William T. Kerr
President and Chief Executive Officer: Stephen M. Lacy

In Memoriam: E.T. Meredith III (1933–2003)

All of us at Meredith® Books are dedicated to providing you with information and ideas to enhance your home. We welcome your comments and suggestions. Write to us at: Meredith Books, Home Decorating and Design Editorial Department, 1716 Locust St., Des Moines, IA 50309-3023.

Contents

A wide ledge on the custom tub surround expands storage and display space. Windows that open to a sheltered tree-filled yard offer ventilation, natural light, and idyllic views.

Bath Design Guide

Bringing Your Beautiful Bath to Life

Exciting new bath fixtures and configurations are a dynamic trend.

People have enjoyed the mental and physical benefits of warm flowing water ever since the first hot spring was encountered. Archaeologists report that wealthy Babylonians and Egyptians installed indoor showers—shallow tubs they stood in while servants poured warm water over them. Ancient Romans, the world's first master plumbers, built indoor latrines next door to public bathhouses, creating what were perhaps the first compartmentalized bathrooms.

If your own bathroom hasn't been updated since Caesar crossed the Rubicon, you're probably considering a renovation. But while "ancient" fixtures and avocado-hue tile are perfectly good reasons for desiring a change, reviving a tired bathroom isn't the only rationale to consider when remodeling or adding a bathroom. In fact there are a host of excellent reasons.

Four good reasons to remodel

Plumbing woes. Modern materials and products have greatly increased the lifespan of bathroom fixtures, but no system lasts forever. A bathroom plagued with drips, leaks, poor drainage, noisy pipes, and inadequate water flows needs help. Repairing or replacing only the offending fixture might be enough, but you may miss hidden damage to floors and walls if wetness has been a chronic problem. If so, renovation may be your best option.

Safety issues. Building codes have reduced the danger of mixing water and electricity, but many older bathrooms are unsafe. Crowded bathrooms lead to bumps and scrapes, and inadequate ventilation promotes the growth of unhealthy mold. Resolving these issues with a bathroom makeover can improve the well-being of every family member.

Cramped quarters. When more than one or two people need a sink, shower, or toilet, everyone feels stressed. If your home's bathrooms are in high demand, adding a partial or full bath may improve dispositions.

An attic often provides the ideal spot for a new bathroom because it is less expensive than building an addition to the house. Work with a professional to ensure ceiling heights meet building codes.

State-of-the-art technologies like this hands-free faucet make saving water comfortable and automatic.

Smart investment. Bathroom remodels traditionally are among the better investments in your home, returning an average of 80 to 90 percent of their cost. If your bathrooms are plainly inadequate compared to those in neighboring houses, a renovation or bath addition may pay back more than its cost when it comes time to sell.

Perhaps none of these reasons to remodel or add a bath applies to you; there's still no reason to doubt your desire for change. Let your dreams and imagination flow like a soothing shower. You'll find plenty of inspiration and advice in the pages that follow.

Start by exploring all the possibilities for bathrooms in Chapter 1, "Explore Your Options." If your bath is too cramped for the family, check out the practical and stylish family baths. In need of an improved master bath? Look at the soothing spaces featured here. Be ready when guests come for short visits by indulging in the fresh ideas for powder rooms. And check out the latest concepts for kids' baths and spalike retreats.

The right bath for you is almost as much about style as it is function. In Chapter 2, "Style Influences," you'll explore a range of looks from traditional to contemporary. You'll also find the latest trends in cottage, fresh country, and world-influenced designs.

In Chapter 3, "Bath Design Basics," a critical component of successful bathroom remodeling projects is discussed: Ensuring the floor plan for your new bath allows enough room for comfortable use of the fixtures. In addition an overview of universal design, safety, and green building considerations helps ensure that the new bath will serve you and your family well over the years.

Chapter 4, "Plan the Project," helps you determine which type of project—facelift, renovation, enlarging a bath, converting another space, or an addition—will best meet your needs and your budget.

The flooring, walls, ceiling, and countertops are the largest areas in the bath. In Chapter 5, "Surfaces," you'll see a range of options for these surface materials, along with suggestions for selecting materials that look great and perform well in the bathroom.

In Chapter 6, "Fixtures," you'll encounter some of the important components in a bathroom. Learn about sinks and faucets, tubs, showers and showerheads, and toilets and bidets. A rundown of the latest fixture materials, plus information about steam showers, easy-clean bathrooms, low-flow fixtures, and more, helps you make smart decisions.

Chapter 7, "Cabinetry & Storage," helps you plan the size, style, and placement of cabinets, shelves, niches, nooks, hooks, and other storage accessories. Your bath is sure to remain a restful spot if you follow the handy recommendations for effective storage.

Move on to Chapter 8, "Lighting & Comfort Systems," to discover how to make the bath as comfortable as possible with the right ventilation and heating. Explore suggestions for lighting schemes that match the functions of the bath.

After you've explored a plethora of possibilities for the bath, take the first step to make it a reality with Chapter 9, "Realize Your Dreams." Here you'll find tips to survive the remodeling process and understand the stages and timelines of your project. Learn the ins and outs of working with professionals in design and remodeling fields and understand what's crucial when it's time to evaluate bids, estimates, and contracts.

Consult Chapter 10, "Resources," for names and contact information of some of the many organizations and associations involved in residential remodeling projects. Learn the definitions of helpful terms you'll use when discussing the bath project with professionals.

This vanity, with inset-panel doors and a quartz-surface top, conveys a vintage look enhanced by glass knobs, nickel sconces, and a gilded mirror. Jerusalem limestone floors, mustard-color walls, and the cream hue of the painted vanity complete a soothing palette.

Soothing neutral hues define this
well-appointed master bath. The
painted vanity blends with the tone
of the tumbled marble wall tiles.

CHAPTER 1

Explore Your Options

Assess Your Needs, Basic Bath Layouts,
Remodeling Options, Setting a Budget, Planning Basics

Craving innovative design? Take cues from this handsome vanity, which offers standard counter and storage space in front of a backsplash made of Brazilian cherrywood slats.

Once reserved for the most mundane matters and light reading, the bathroom has grown in size and ambition. Twin vanities enable couples to trade schedules during the morning rush hour. Jetted tubs provide relief for aching muscles. Steam showers and saunas melt away stress. Luxuriously designed fixtures have become objets d'art in these 100-square-foot private galleries. The modern privy plays almost as many roles as the kitchen.

The goal of this chapter is to help you sort through all of these potential functions and assess which ones are most important to you. Start by analyzing your needs. Next look at a variety of layouts, trends, and remodeling options to see which ones might best serve you. Then consider the financial side of things. Finally, take a peek at six common bathroom styles to figure out which best suits your needs.

ASSESS YOUR NEEDS

Sometimes the simplest way to figure out what you want in life is to look critically at what you already have. This approach works for cars, careers, and potential spouses—so why not a bathroom? Of course it's not always easy to perform such an assessment. Little things that loom large, such as a chip in the sink, may keep you from noticing, for example, that the toilet your builder installed 10 years ago is more appropriately sized for an elementary school restroom. If you want a thorough assessment, you'll need to invest a bit of time. The chart below will get you started.

Design Tip

To get the best assessment of your needs, record your likes and dislikes. Buy a notebook and pen and keep them in the bathroom where you'll see them every time you wash your hands. Whenever the muse strikes, note what you like and don't like. Encourage other family members to do the same. Within a week or two, you'll be in a better position to explain to your architect, designer, or builder what you want and—equally important—what you don't want.

SIZING UP YOUR BATHROOM	CURRENT BATH	PRIORITY (1, 2, 3)
Room Size and Layout		
Two people fit comfortably in this bathroom at the same time.	☐ Yes ☐ No	_____
Opening the main door is likely to hit someone at the sink or on the toilet.	☐ Yes ☐ No	_____
Frequent traffic jams occur in or near the bathroom.	☐ Yes ☐ No	_____
Enough room is on the counter for the items you like to keep there.	☐ Yes ☐ No	_____
Space exists for a hamper, scale, towel warmer, or other extras you'd like.	☐ Yes ☐ No	_____
Fixtures and Amenities		
The tub has the capacity and shape for relaxing soaks.	☐ Yes ☐ No	_____
A convenient place exists to shave or apply makeup.	☐ Yes ☐ No	_____
The sink is a good size, shape, and height.	☐ Yes ☐ No	_____
The toilet is a comfortable size and height.	☐ Yes ☐ No	_____
A place exists to lay a towel and robe near the tub.	☐ Yes ☐ No	_____
There is plenty of light throughout the day.	☐ Yes ☐ No	_____
This bathroom is safe for young children and people with disabilities.	☐ Yes ☐ No	_____
You would like more electrical outlets near the sink or mirror.	☐ Yes ☐ No	_____
There is a radio, sound system, or TV.	☐ Yes ☐ No	_____
Noticeable scratches or damage exists on counters or cabinets.	☐ Yes ☐ No	_____
Ventilation is sufficient to keep mirrors from fogging.	☐ Yes ☐ No	_____
The shower is a comfortable size.	☐ Yes ☐ No	_____
Location		
The bathroom is convenient to the bedrooms it serves.	☐ Yes ☐ No	_____
The path from the bedroom to the bathroom passes through a living area.	☐ Yes ☐ No	_____
When the door is open, the toilet is visible from living areas.	☐ Yes ☐ No	_____

Design that meets specialized needs—providing for wheelchair access in front of a vanity, for example—does not mean compromising on style.

BASIC BATH LAYOUTS

Now that you know what you need (and want) in your new bathroom, it's time to find inspiration so you can determine what your bath layout will actually look like. Watching decorating shows and browsing through magazines and books like this one are great places to begin generating ideas and information. The baths you see may have markedly different characteristics from your own, but they can yield creativity-provoking ideas on everything from materials to colors that you can apply to your project.

For more ideas spend time in home centers and plumbing supply houses, attend home shows, and explore the nicest real estate open houses in town. Gather brochures, take pictures, and organize your ideas any way that makes sense to you.

Nowhere to go but up

While you are gathering ideas for your new bath, begin the process of thinking about the amount of space (and money) you'll need to devote to the project. A good place to begin space planning is with a minimum-size floor plan. That way you can add space incrementally to accommodate the features you want. If you start with a set size, you risk trying to squeeze too much in or having wasted space left over. On the opposite page are six basic minimum bathroom layouts (showing interior measurements), along with notes that will help you understand where best to start the process of expanding on them.

Design Tip

Start a bathroom idea folder early in your planning process. File examples of bathrooms and fixtures that you like as well as those you don't like. Both will help you to communicate your vision to design professionals. Also save all versions of sketches and floor plans.

Regardless of bath size consider door clearances. This bath provides ample space between the open glass shower door and the vanity on an adjacent wall.

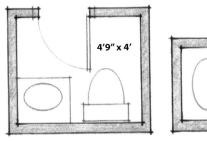

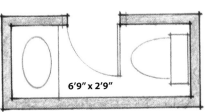

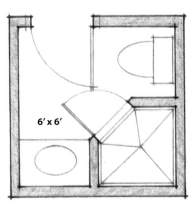

The half bath

Minimum-size half baths are adequate for guest use. Their small size may make them difficult to maintain, however. Because of the tight spacing, you'll need to clean around the toilet on hands and knees. The version that is close to square is less likely to produce collisions in a no-knock situation. It's also the better layout if the family uses this bathroom regularly because you can extend a narrow section of counter above the toilet tank if you install a low-profile model. Enlarging either layout even slightly will eliminate many of these challenges.

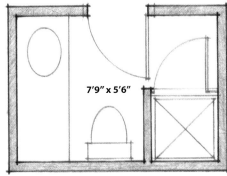

The three-quarter bath

Installing a shower rather than a tub allows you to squeeze a full-service bathroom into a smaller space. Either of these layouts would pair well with a teenager's bedroom, a guest room, or in a tight spot such as an attic conversion. The horizontal layout assumes a 30-inch-square shower stall. Though widely available, this size makes for an uncomfortable experience. If possible, opt for a minimum 36-inch-square unit. The square layout is still a bit cramped, especially around the toilet, but is a much better configuration than the rectangular layout.

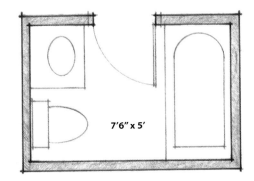

The full bath

Both of these configurations work well for kids' bathrooms, especially if the children are young, or for guest baths. For adults who use the bath regularly, the limited storage space may be a challenge. The compartmentalized version works best, as the pocket doors enable two adults to share space (although it will be cozy). The majority of tubs will fit along a 5-foot-long wall, but some oversize tubs require an extra 6 to 12 inches of length.

REMODELING OPTIONS

Why undertake a down-to-the-studs remodeling if less-expensive moves will achieve the same results? Though your heart may be set on an addition, you might get a better outcome with a simpler approach. Before you leap into action, take time to consider your options.

Give a facelift

A facelift typically involves changes to decorative surfaces. It's a good option for updating a bathroom's appearance or adding value inexpensively. Common bathroom facelift options include:

Freshening the walls. Revive tired walls with a fresh coat of paint, a few rolls of wallpaper, or beaded-board wainscoting. Stick with light tones, especially in small bathrooms.

Laying a new floor. Upgrading from vinyl to ceramic tile is a popular move and offers the option of radiant underfloor heating—a real plus now and when it comes time to sell. If you like the look of wood or stone but don't want to spend a fortune, consider laminate flooring.

Reviving a vanity. Replace the countertop with one of the new synthetic stone materials for a luxe look that's maintenance free. Or refinish or replace the cabinet doors.

Installing new accessories. Trade old towel bars, soap holders, and other accoutrements for stylish new models.

Add new fixtures

Swapping fixtures can make your bath more stylish, provide better performance, and reduce your water and energy consumption. Consider new fixtures if existing ones are performing poorly or are unsightly or undersize. Here are possible changes:

Sink and faucet. A new sink often means a new countertop and faucet too. Purchase the best quality you can afford.

Toilet. The best new models look fantastic, are one-flush reliable, and use less water.

Tub. You'll find a vast array of materials and colors to choose from, but if space is tight, you'll probably need a standard 5-foot-long model.

Lighting or ventilation. Eye-level light fixtures are best for even illumination. Look for Energy Star-rated fixtures, which cost less to operate. When replacing a ventilation fan, choose one that has a low noise rating.

Consider new fixtures, such as a vintage-look soaking tub in place of a standard shower-tub combo, to create serious style without major remodeling. Replacing large fixtures requires careful planning. Make sure you can get them into the house before you buy.

Leave no space unexplored if you're looking to expand a crowded bathroom. An under-the-stairs niche like this one allows toilet placement outside the bath's main traffic zone.

A 4-foot-deep bumpout is enough to create a nook for a generous spa tub. Because the floor is cantilevered, no new foundation is required. Bumpouts can also be used on upper floors. Because of the loads involved, however, be sure a construction engineer signs off on your plans.

A powder room requires only a pedestal sink and toilet. With some creativity even a minimum-size half bath can fit into the space a closet once occupied.

Expand the space

Sometimes you can save a cramped bathroom by expanding into space borrowed from an adjacent room, closet, or hallway. Use the extra square footage for:

- A makeup counter and seat.
- An extra sink. Install a twin vanity or a separate sink outside the main bath area.
- An oversize tub or separate shower.
- A sauna or steam room.

Design a new bathroom

Perhaps you've increased your family size and one bathroom isn't enough any more. Consider:

Adapting existing space. Study your home's floor plan for space that you could use as a bathroom. You might be able to tuck a powder room under a stairway or in a closet or expand into unfinished space above a garage.

Adding new space. Although this is often the most expensive option, there are ways to control costs. To add some elbowroom consider a bumpout, a minor addition that doesn't incur the expense of a new foundation. If you're converting attic space, a good option is to expand into a dormer. Regardless of the approaches you consider, discuss your situation with a design or building professional.

SETTING A BUDGET

Eventually your bath remodeling blueprints translate into green dollars. A workable budget usually is a compromise between all the great things you imagine for your finished project and what you're willing and able to spend to achieve your goals. At this point your first priority is to set limits for the total amount of money you will spend. As a guide, make two lists. One list will include everything you consider essential for your new space. The other list will comprise the extras, the amenities you'd like to have if there's money left after you pay for essentials. Once you develop your budget, stay committed to it. A commitment to your bottom line will help when difficult cost-cutting decisions come knocking.

Cost-Saving Strategies

Your budget should include all of the essentials for your project, but it is possible to save money with these steps:

Simplify the design. Look at premium architectural features, such as curved walls or ceiling treatments, or high-end fixtures such as saunas and whirlpools. Separate frills from essentials.

Substitute less-expensive materials. Great looks come in a wide range of prices. Some materials—such as certain natural stone tiles—can be expensive. Research flooring alternatives that replicate the look of natural stone; you may find the look for substantially less per square foot.

Tackle some of the work yourself. Demolition, painting, tiling, and cleanup are popular do-it-yourself jobs. Consider handling minor surface regrading and the cleanup and finish work, such as painting and installing trim.

Smart remodeling choices in the bathroom can increase the value of your home—and make the money borrowed to complete the remodel worth it. This bath's neutral-hue mosaic tiles, furniture-style vanity, and limestone flooring impart timeless elegance.

Bid basics

As you finalize your ideas and move toward construction, request bids from contractors and other professionals you're considering to complete the work. Convey your goals and budget to the professionals involved in the project. Once you receive bids, add a 5 to 10 percent cushion to the total figure to cover cost overruns and changes to your plans that may occur after construction has begun. (For more information on obtaining bids, turn to page 193.)

What it's worth

One of the most expensive mistakes you can make is to overimprove. Buyers shy away from homes that are substantially more expensive than similar homes in the neighborhood, so the house might take much longer to sell. You could even find yourself "upside down"— owing more to the bank than you can get in a sale.

A simple rule can help you avoid this trap. Beware if the adjusted value of your home—the current value plus the cost of remodeling—will be more than 20 to 25 percent above the average for comparable homes in your area. A bath remodel alone usually doesn't reach this tipping point, but it's worth doing the math.

Don't want to spend a fortune expanding a small bath? Look for spacesaving design tricks instead. A shallow vanity, wide mirror, and tall cabinet mounted above the tub help this compact bath feel bigger and more functional.

Sources of Money

Cash. It's the simplest way to pay for your bathroom transformation. Write a check or use your credit card and pay off the monthly charges.

Savings. Borrow from yourself to save the hassle (and expense) of paying interest to a lending institution.

Home equity loan. This type of loan borrows against the equity you've built in your home. The rates are fixed, so payment each month over the term of the loan (generally between 5 and 30 years) remains the same. The amount you can borrow depends on your home's appraised or fair market value and the amount you still owe on any outstanding mortgage loans. The interest paid on this type of loan generally is tax deductible.

Home equity line of credit. This form of revolving credit is based on your home's value and the amount of equity you have. With this loan you have the flexibility of borrowing as you go. Interest rates are variable so monthly payments vary.

Refinancing. Taking a cash-out mortgage loan allows you to refinance your mortgage for a higher overall amount than what you owe on your home. The amount depends on your home's accumulated equity and value. Interest rates are lower than with home equity loans but expect to pay standard closing costs.

Low-cost improvement loans. Available in many cities for developing or historic neighborhoods or for people in low-income situations, these loans are sometimes forgivable. Contact your local building code official, city planner, or historical society to learn more about programs that help cut the cost of financing your endeavor.

PLANNING BASICS: FAMILY BATHS

For its size the family bathroom is probably the hardest-working space in your home. In many households this room sees action throughout the day. It needs to withstand high humidity, tracked-in grime, and standing water that puddles on floors and counters. Unlike the master bath, which typically caters to one or two adults of similar age and needs, the family bathroom accommodates everyone from preschool kids to preening teens to elderly guests. The need for versatility makes designing one a challenge.

This section lays out the elements to consider when planning a family bathroom. Many of the principles apply to master suites and half baths as well.

Size and layout

Most home buyers want at least one bathtub, and the family bath is the best location for it if your house will have only one full bath. Although a tub, sink, and toilet can squeeze into a 5×7-foot space, a 6×8-foot (or larger) area is desirable in terms of comfort, storage, and safety.

If you are renovating a minimum-size bath, consider annexing adjacent space, expanding into a hallway, or bumping out an exterior wall several feet. Bear in mind that a bathroom can go beyond the lines of a simple square or rectangle. By incorporating a portion of an adjacent closet, for example, you can create an alcove large enough for a tub.

To better serve multiple users on hectic mornings, consider a compartmentalized bath. The most common arrangement is to sequester the toilet in its own compartment. But a more useful arrangement for a family bathroom may be to put the tub and toilet each in its own compartment so multiple users can be in the bathroom at once.

This double vanity, which fits the traditional style of the rest of the home, features a space-efficient corner design that's suited to sharing. To oblige users of all ages, the circular mirrors above the vanity tilt. The two sinks hang slightly lower than standard height, but the center section of the vanity is set several inches higher.

A combination tub and shower is a smart choice for a family bath. This model, which boasts a center-mount showerhead, sculptural spigot, and whirlpool tub, is primed to pamper.

Comfort and convenience

Because it must provide for a range of users, the family bath needs to take a multipronged approach to keeping its users satisfied. At the most basic level, this means walls, floors, countertops, and cabinetry that are durable, easy to clean, and low-maintenance.

To maximize flexibility and make the most efficient use of space, plan on a mix of closed and open storage at several levels. Use the lower-level areas for items that kids need to access, such as clean towels and extra rolls of toilet paper, and higher areas for cleaning supplies and other items that you want to keep out of reach. (If you have very young children, keep hazardous items in childproof storage.) One thing you probably shouldn't store in the bathroom is medicine; many are sensitive to the light, heat, and humidity. Finally, don't forget to designate a place to stash dirty laundry and towels.

The features that apply to children may be different from those that apply to adults, but ideally both sets of considerations should coexist comfortably. For example, rather than placing a child's step stool in front of the vanity, consider a step that pulls out from the toe-kick. Likewise you can install towel bars at two levels so that everyone has access. And a low bench assists all ages when dressing and putting on shoes.

Comfort features for the family bath range from proper ventilation to well-planned lighting. For added warmth include an overhead heat lamp, a small heater tucked into the toe space of a vanity, or radiant-heat flooring. Keep decor gender- and age-neutral.

Side-by-side baths connected via a pocket door allow family members privacy when needed and access to shared fixtures when the door is open.

Putty-color cabinetry and durable granite countertops combine in this bath, which won't go out of style any time soon. Undercounter storage accommodates family members young and old; a large basket keeps towels handy so kids don't have to rummage through cabinets.

PLANNING BASICS: MASTER BATHS

Because it serves one or two adults, the master bathroom offers the opportunity for greater personalization, an expanded palette of materials and features, and luxury amenities. Based on trends in new housing, a well-appointed master bath is often a smart long-term investment.

Here are some key considerations to include in your planning process.

Size and layout

A 6×8-foot space works for two adults if a tub, toilet, and single vanity are all you need; allow about 6×10 feet if a double vanity is part of the plan. Any additional features increase the amount of space required as does an oversize tub (larger than the standard 30×60-inch models).

Compartmentalization improves a master bath, as it does a family bath. In this case, however, separating the toilet alone makes more sense because privacy in the tub or shower isn't as much of an issue. An increasingly popular arrangement is to spread the fixtures over a larger portion of the master suite. For example, you might install an extra single vanity in the master bedroom or dressing area or a soaking tub in the bedroom, leaving the shower in the master bath. Beware, however, that the more unusual the arrangement, the greater the chance buyers won't like it.

Because it partners with a bedroom, the master bath also is often allied with other functional areas. The classic example is an adjacent walk-in closet or, if there's room, a separate dressing area. Locating a dressing area between the bedroom and bath provides a measure of sound insulation, although it also risks creating an obstacle course between the bedroom and bathroom.

Ample counterspace between sinks and plenty of storage space for each person make this master vanity convenient for two people.

With enough space and the right location, master baths allow for luxurious details. The courtyard shower makes this a true indoor-outdoor bath. Fluted glass and stone add to the natural aura.

A fresh take on the traditional dual vanity, this cubical two-basin unit serves as the hub of the bath. Mirrored medicine cabinets mounted to a steel pole offer innovative, adjustable storage.

A new trend in high-end homes is the "morning kitchen," a small room adjacent to the bedroom outfitted with a bar sink, mini refrigerator, beverage maker, and even a small table. If space is available, and the plumbing and wiring can be tied into the bath's, adding this feature will be reasonably economical.

Fixtures

Master baths are the ideal place to work in a special feature. It's hard enough to get kids to wash their hands after using the bathroom, so it's doubtful that a bidet in the family bath would get much use. Put it in a master bath, however, and you may have a good fit.

A vast new world of interesting and artistic fixtures awaits you. Air-bath tubs, which surround bathers with effervescent bubbles, are the latest innovation promising to knock the whirlpool tub off its perch as the ultimate in bathing luxury. Multiple-head showers allow two people to shower as comfortably as one. And vessel sinks, which look like ceramic bowls set on a counter, provide a seemingly unlimited choice of shapes, sizes, and colors to top the modern vanity.

A less traditional but very welcome category of fixtures includes media such as TVs, radios, or sound systems. Be sure that electronics, unless designed for wet environments, are kept away from water splashes.

Finally, a detailed lighting plan will do much to enhance the soothing aura of your master bath. Put general lighting on dimmers so you can create a mood or provide softer light at night. Consider task lighting for common activities, such as grooming, shaving, and even reading. A comfortable master bath is a haven, a place in which to retreat and recharge.

Design Tip

Rather than using standard cabinetry, consider creating a sink vanity out of a dresser. A cabinetmaker can cut a hole in the top of the dresser to fit a drop-in sink. Coat the remaining wooden surface with polyurethane to protect it from water and moisture. If space permits you can incorporate a matching chest of drawers for storage.

Storage

When it comes to storage in the master bath, one size does not fit all. Instead of taking the conventional approach—doubling up on vanities, for example—consider each user separately. Some users prefer drawers for storage, while others like shelves. Deep cabinets with pullout drawers might work for one partner's plethora of hair care products, while the other may need only a small basket for a bottle of shampoo. In other words let use and preferences dictate the design of the master bath, not simply a desire to create mirror images of each person's personal space.

Design Tip

Converting a large closet or a small spare bedroom into a dressing room may be a smart move if the master bathroom barely offers space for the essential fixtures. Think about traffic flow and storage needs as you consider the best location for your dressing room.

This floor plan pushes function to the perimeter, leaving an atriumlike space in the middle of the room below a 10-foot ceiling. The shower enclosure is on the left, and the doorway straight ahead leads to one of two walk-in closets.

PLANNING BASICS: POWDER ROOMS AND HALF BATHS

Although the terms often are used interchangeably, half baths and powder rooms are two distinct rooms. A half bath includes a sink and toilet intended primarily for family use; a powder room is a half bath intended to serve visitors as well as family members.

Here are the key considerations for planning a half bath, along with a few special suggestions that apply particularly to powder rooms.

Size and layout

The smallest reasonable half bath measures roughly 3×6 feet if the sink and toilet face each other or 4×5 feet if they share the long wall. To increase the comfort factor, add 1 foot to the shorter dimension. A window does much to reduce the claustrophobic feeling that can arise in such a small space.

For a powder room the most important consideration is its location. It should be accessible from each of the main living areas but not directly visible from those areas. A location near the entry or entry hallway is desirable.

Materials and fixtures

For half baths that cater to the entire family, select materials that are durable and easy to maintain. A gently used powder room, however, is an opportunity to make a memorable impression on guests. Consider decorating it with more delicate, stylish materials, such as attractive wall and window coverings and perhaps even a sculptural vessel sink. Whatever your personal style, powder rooms are ideal for displaying your preferences.

A smaller powder room will feel less crowded with a pedestal sink than with a vanity, though the reduction in storage capacity limits the room's usefulness for family members. One fixture not to skimp on is the toilet. Choose a model with a larger, elongated bowl and powerful flush mechanism to minimize the odds of unsightly residue.

Be sure to budget for good lighting. Your guests will appreciate a flattering glow, as will family members ducking in for a quick primp. Wall sconces flanking a mirror convey a cozy, living room feel—much better than the harsh shadows cast by a standard ceiling fixture.

Dressed in white this half bath makes the most of light from a window above the vessel sink. A narrow section of countertop extends above the toilet tank, making it perfect for rolled-up hand towels.

Here's an innovative answer to a too-small powder room space: The sink pulls out from the wall on drawer hinges.

PLANNING BASICS: KIDS' BATHS

The challenge in planning a children's bath lies in creating a space that younger kids can enjoy while providing easy opportunities to upgrade as they grow older. The key is to use timeless fixtures and materials, then set an age-appropriate theme with easily changed decorative features such as paint finishes, stencils, artwork, light fixtures, shower curtains, and bath linens.

Size and layout

A children's bath need not be larger or smaller than a typical family bath. Even the youngest children will grow to adult size in just a few years. If two or more children will use the bathroom at once, consider compartmentalizing the toilet and including a double vanity.

One accommodation to consider: lowering the height of light switches to 36 to 42 inches from the floor. This makes them equally accessible to adults and children. Just be sure that the height and location you choose are acceptable under your local building codes.

Materials and fixtures

Kid-friendly materials are rugged, easy to clean and maintain, and textured to prevent falls. Choose scrubbable paint or tile for the walls and nonslip tile or vinyl for the floor. Look for countertops with smooth, rounded edges (those made from solid-surfacing are a good option). If you are a stickler for cleanliness, consider materials that incorporate antibacterial protection, such as some engineered stone countertops.

Resist the urge to install child-size toilets and sinks that will have to be replaced as the kids grow or when you decide to sell the house. Instead make it easier for children to use standard fixtures. Child-size toilet seats and nonskid step stools help kids navigate safely and comfortably.

Avoid installing shower doors on the tub if your kids are too young to bathe on their own. Shower curtains that can be pushed out of the way make it much easier for an adult to assist a young child.

Starfish and sea horses turn simple drawer and door pulls into kid-friendly decorative elements.

Safety Matters

Before kids splish-splash in the bath, ensure that the room is safe for get-clean fun. The following are easy, inexpensive safety precautions worth taking today. For more information on bathroom safety, turn to page 85.

Install antiscald devices on sinks and tubs, and turn the water heater down to 120 degrees Fahrenheit to prevent burns.

Secure lower cabinets and drawers with press-release latches, spring latches, or locks.

Keep the toilet seat down with a toilet lid latch.

Use mini shower mats or tub treads to prevent slips and falls in the tub.

Place cushioned covers over the tub faucet to soften edges in case kids slip.

Install quick-access privacy locks on doors so you can get in quickly if needed.

Use plastic (rather than glass) for tumblers and other accessories.

rub a dub dub • ru...ub ...b dub • rub a dub ...rub

Color-washed walls and stenciled accents create a cheerful theme bath that's easy to update when little ones grow. If rugs are used on bathroom floors, be sure they are secured with nonslip backing.

Soaking in a whirlpool tub in front of a fireplace is a luxury that's hard to beat. Gleaming surfaces and access to the outdoors up the spa factor even more.

PLANNING BASICS: SPA BATHS

Why travel to a spa when you can create a haven for rest and relaxation in your own home? Whether you are seeking hedonistic pleasure or a therapeutic experience, bathrooms that have it all—saunas, steam showers, and heated floors, among other indulgences—make an ideal retreat.

Size and layout

It's possible to build a spa bath in the same space as a traditional full bath, but remember that the more features and fixtures you incorporate, the more space you'll need. Regardless of size and layout, check the structural underpinnings of your space. Deep soaking tubs may call for beefed-up floors and larger water supply lines to fill them in a reasonable amount of time. Your contractor, designer, and fixture suppliers can help you determine which structural, plumbing, or electrical upgrades you might need.

Materials and fixtures

Materials used in luxury baths range from shimmery glass tiles and smooth expanses of marble to slabs of natural stone or cabinets custom-made from exotic wood. Such choices are a matter of personal preference (and budget of course). The goal is to create a personalized space that's focused on the needs and wants of its inhabitants.

When it comes to selecting spalike fixtures, the options for home use are expanding. Odds are you can find the

A high ceiling punctuated by a chandelier reigns over this spacious bath, which combines the comfort of luxury fixtures with the style of marble floors adorned with onyx insets.

elements to complete your luxury bath. The sidebar, below, describes some options to consider. For more on luxury fixtures and spa trends, turn to pages 152–153 and 182–183.

Can't-Miss Luxury Features

Here's the lowdown on some of the spa features and fixtures you'll find at your bath supply house or home center:

Relaxation tubs. Jet or whirlpool tubs provide an invigorating massage. Air baths inject tiny bubbles into the water for a gentler massage. And for smaller bathrooms, a narrow but deep soaking tub lets you relax in warm water from toe to chin. Add a wide waterfall faucet and a hand wand for rinsing yourself and cleaning the tub.

Want even more spalike benefits? Chromatherapy systems are one of the latest innovations. Submerged lights transition through a specific range of colors, an experience that adherents claim provides health benefits including mood enhancement and stress reduction.

Shower power. If space is tight, outfit a tub with dual showerheads on opposite walls so two people can shower at the same time. Other options include sunflower-size rain dome heads and full-body units that spray from head to toe.

Steam and more. Steam generators, most often installed in shower stalls, provide a quick way to achieve total body relaxation. For maximum benefit include a long bench for resting while the steam does its work. Consider including a built-in whirlpool foot bath inside the shower stall too.

Bonus features. Start with an electric or hydronic towel warmer, then add subfloor heating under a tile or stone floor. Include a CD player or other system for channeling in soothing sounds or smooth jazz to complete your bathroom retreat.

DESIGN GALLERY
Trends

It's worth noting the difference between fads and trends. The pink fixtures of the '50s faded fast, but the master bath setup introduced a few years later is still around. Check out these trends that have real staying power.

1. Made for more than soaking your cares away, a freestanding tub naturally becomes a dramatic, sculptural focal point.

2. Look for showers that have it all. This two-person version boasts full-body nozzle sprays, a large-diameter rain head, and heated limestone flooring.

3. Shapely sinks perched on the countertop garner serious style points whether they're sturdy square basins or delicate vessels like these.

4. Sleek, discreet toilets resemble hatboxes more than commodes while retaining the comfort and function you expect.

5. Forget basic built-in vanities. Freestanding pieces look more like antique furniture than bathroom necessities.

6. Say goodbye to boring faucets. It's all about high-shine geometric design now.

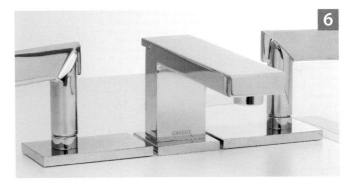

A neutral palette makes this traditional
retreat the perfect spot for a peaceful bath.

CHAPTER 2

Style Influences

Find Your Personal Style, Elements of Design, Tradtional Style, Contemporary Style, Fresh Country Style, World Style

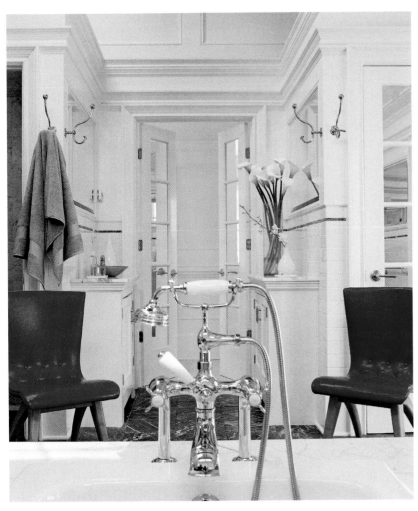

This master bath uses symmetry to a mirror-image degree. French doors open to twin cabinets, mirrors, towel hooks, and red chairs.

Just as a soak in a bubbly whirlpool tub eases tired muscles, the look of your bathroom should relax and renew—whether you're waking up to start the day or winding down after hours on the run. With the right choices, a renovated bath becomes an expression of your style while it caters to your needs.

Where do you begin to determine what colors, textures, materials, and accessories appeal to you? Perhaps you're leaning toward a clean-line retreat with soothing colors and sleek fixtures. Or maybe a traditional bath with warm wood tones and classic detailing is more your taste. The baths in this chapter give you a sample of traditional, contemporary, cottage, fresh country, and world styles. Use the information and ideas that resonate with you as a starting point. Which style and form your bathroom takes after that is up to you.

FIND YOUR PERSONAL STYLE

Each bathroom in this chapter meets the personal needs and interests of a particular homeowner. You'll want your bathroom to suit your particular needs as well. As you peruse the photos, note what you like and don't like. When fashioning your ideal bath, knowing what you don't care for is as important as articulating what you want to include.

If you are uncertain about which look is right for you and your family, touring this chapter—as well as the rest of the book—is an excellent starting point. Remember that the bath is your personal space, so feel free to mix and match, borrow from, and combine the looks you see here to create a room that is uniquely yours.

To devise a soothing, spalike retreat, for example, choose serene colors and tile or stone finishes that make for a smooth, polished look. If textured warmth is more your idea of comfort, make room for a terry cloth-covered stool and an antique-look furniture-style vanity. Or perhaps you're hoping to continue the period style of the rest of your home in the bath. In an Arts and Crafts-style home this may mean installing wide white trim around doors and windows and white-painted beaded-board wainscoting on the wall. The examples in this chapter touch on general styles in bathroom design, but don't feel limited by what you see. Use your imagination!

Design Tip

A certified bath designer can help turn your scribbled notes about likes and dislikes into the bath of your dreams. Contact the National Kitchen and Bath Association at 800/843-6522 or visit nkba.org to find a certified bath designer in your area.

A custom mirror rimmed with antiqued glass and rosette details accents this vanity and fits the era of the 1935 Tudor-style home. Antique sconces lend a touch of vintage glamour to the vanity area.

A little elegance goes a long way as this modern metropolitan bath proves. Mosaic tiles, Art Deco geometrics, and sensuous furnishings combine for one-of-a-kind style.

A limited range of colors and surfaces—glass panels, a gray limestone countertop, and Carrara marble tiles—complement the simple shape of this small guest bath.

ELEMENTS OF DESIGN

Color, texture, line, and pattern are the key elements of room design. Learn how each element functions so you can create a cohesive, welcoming space.

Color

Color sets the mood. Reds and oranges create warmth, and blues and greens are typically soothing hues. Bringing color into the bathroom can be as simple and inexpensive as choosing colorful bath towels and rugs or painting the walls. Want to go even bolder? Many companies manufacture building materials and fixtures in various colors. Dyed concrete floors and countertops, painted porcelain sinks, colorful cabinetry, and even sunny yellow bathroom fixtures are options. If a bold color scheme tempts you, consider whether the look will appeal to you for long. Changing the color of more permanent elements is more complicated and expensive than repainting the walls.

Texture

Texture is more than tactile, it's also visual. For instance, rough-hewn stone on walls or floors conveys rustic appeal, and the smooth lines of marble countertops exude tradition. For balance try juxtaposing textures. Mix smooth metal with honed stone or wood look-alikes with sleek ceramics. Or consider interesting, low-commitment ways to include textural touches—brushed-chrome faucets, a freestanding vanity constructed from distressed wood, or fluffy bath towels are all possibilities.

Simplicity is a virtue, especially for tiny powder rooms. Here an elegantly curved apron conceals the plumbing but is left open below to enhance the sense of space.

Line

Lines are pivotal in bath composition. Consider how the edges and corners of objects such as sinks, vanities, and windows lend distinction to the composition of your bath. Rectilinear lines, like those found in shoji screens, are common in Asian-inspired baths. And strong horizontal lines dominate Craftsman-style design.

Pattern

Patterns can be regular (lending stability to design) or random (creating energy and interest). If you want your bath to be a calming retreat, be sure to use patterns in a symmetrical and balanced way. Choose patterns carefully to avoid overwhelming a space. Pattern may appear on wallpaper, rugs, window treatments, and shower curtains. Or it may be more subtle, showing up in the arrangement of tiles on a backsplash or floor.

Art in the Bath

Reveal your artistic sensibilities and add serious style to your bath by hanging framed artwork and displaying vessels or handcarved sculptures.

Hang a large oil painting in an ornate frame over the tub in a nod to an old world-look. You can use inexpensive black and white prints or botanical reproductions to add flair and drama too—but don't hang valuable works on paper in the bathroom. Steam and moisture will ruin them.

Group the artwork to give collections more importance and interest. Or stick with one distinctive piece and leave the rest of the walls bare—the sculptural style of many bathroom fixtures is art in itself.

Choose glazed ceramic vases or handblown glass pieces, moisture-resistant artwork, to decorate with.

A crisp palette of black and white defines this vintage-inspired bath. Reflective surfaces throughout—glossy tiles, mirrors, glass, polished chrome—enhance the clean look.

Linen-color cabinets and sandy-hue ceramic tiles steer this master bath toward a nautical theme. Above the vanity area, maritime wallpaper and a large model boat further the seaside style.

TRADITIONAL STYLE

The classic features of traditional decor never go out of style. Whether it's a tiny first-floor powder room or an expansive master bath, a room dressed in tradition possesses an air of graciousness, elegance, and timelessness. Inspired by the European opulence of the 18th century, traditional style has long been known for gilded finishes and floral fabrics, as well as enduring accents such as porcelain, gold, and silver. Its furniture-style cabinets, ornate molding, and subdued color schemes may appear formal, but they're key to constructing a comfortable, welcoming space that will last long after trends disappear.

Design Tip

The humidity in a bath can take a toll on fabrics. If your bath will include fabrics and wallpapers, see pages 180–181 to plan for proper ventilation. Save more delicate fabrics for powder rooms where moisture isn't a concern. You can also make window treatments and upholster furnishings with outdoor fabrics that are made to resist water and humidity.

Marble countertops and furniturelike cabinetry are the foundation of traditional style.

This vanity, resembling a piece of freestanding furniture, serves as the room's focal point. The window's white fluted molding and rosettes embody architectural definition.

Period details, such as fluted columns and a combination of dentil and picture frame moldings, lend a vintage feel to this vanity hutch.

Add Architectural Touches

Most trimwork found in homes today derives at least some inspiration from traditional style, with its emphasis on classic proportion and symmetry. Consider using these basic trimwork elements to enhance the style of your bath:

Baseboard trim installed along the bottom of walls, cabinets, and even tub surrounds helps tie the room's elements together.

Crown molding spans the space between the ceiling and the wall and lends detail and character to the room. Built-up crown molding looks best in ornate baths but simpler profiles work almost anywhere. Crown molding may also top upper cabinets. As much as possible, balance the crown molding and base trim.

Wainscoting dresses up the walls and may be topped with a shelf for displaying collectibles or stashing bath items. It's also common in country-style baths.

Cabinet details, such as carved appliqués, corbels, fluted columns, and furniture-style feet, give standard bathroom cabinetry a handcrafted appearance.

Include common elements

The details in a traditional bath may vary (for example, some baths showcase undermount sinks, others feature pedestal units), but there are some common characteristics:

- Symmetrical arrangements of cabinetry and fixtures that create a feeling of balance and order
- Wood, wood-tone, or white-painted cabinets and furniture
- Architectural details such as deep crown moldings, chair rails, wainscoting, and finely crafted woodwork
- Cabinetry with raised panels
- Furniture-style vanities with elevated bottom edges and exposed legs
- Freestanding storage pieces such as armoires
- Windows with muntins
- Natural surface materials such as stone and tile

Attention to details, such as the furniture-style trimwork on the custom cabinetry and marble floors inset with honey onyx, contributes classic elegance to a traditional master bath.

Remember the details

Beyond architectural details and materials that define traditional style, little touches can help turn an ordinary bath into a sanctuary:

- Clean-line and formal window treatments such as Roman shades, shutters, or tailored swags
- Abundant floral or toile fabrics in draperies, vanity skirts, and wallpapers
- Brass or shiny metal accents such as towel rings, faucets, doorknobs, drawer pulls, and mirror frames
- Botanical prints and framed old-world reproductions
- Vintage accessories including sconces, urns, handpainted ceramics, and cut-glass bottles and vases
- Chairs and footstools tailored or upholstered in a brocade or other sumptuous fabric

DESIGN GALLERY
Traditional Details

Traditional baths combine the warm luxury of classic features with stunning good looks culled from individual design sensibilities. The result: The mix of details and symmetry shown here, which is sure to remind you why this look never loses its edge.

1. Traditional style is in the details of this vanity, which includes intricate edging on the marble countertops and custom cabinetry with mini columns and recessed door panels.

2. Shutters, beaded-board wainscoting, and a mix of travertine and tumbled marble exude a light-filled traditional aura.

3. The subtle elegance of a brushed metal tub filler and hand shower mounted on a marble tub deck imparts a classy touch.

4. Clean white wainscoting, mirrors topped with crown molding, porcelain sinks with turned legs, and vintage-inspired faucets and sconces evoke period ambience.

5. A creamy beige marble tub surround provides a place for decor and bathing items to rest. Its elegant curves accent the marble backsplash.

CONTEMPORARY STYLE

Contemporary style is known for its clean lines, wood finishes, and appreciation for modern artistry. This look is meditative in its calm, quiet attitude and often features Asian-inspired influences. A contemporary approach is a natural for the bath, where surfaces are sleek and uncluttered, cabinets and countertops are made of wood and natural stone or tile, and opportunities abound for metal accents in the form of hardware and fixtures.

A long vanity wall combines cast-concrete sinks, round mirrors, and sleek custom cabinets. Abundant storage contains the clutter, a contemporary strength.

Include common elements

Contemporary-style bathrooms have these elements in common:

- Wood-tone built-in cabinets with flat door and drawer fronts, no recessed panels and intricately carved molding
- Stone slabs or tiles, such as slate, limestone, granite, or marble
- Sleek, shapely faucets for the tub, shower, and sink
- Built-in and hidden storage, absence of clutter
- Undermounted tubs in keeping with clean horizontal surfaces
- Glass shower doors
- Hard window treatments, such as shutters, blinds, or frosted glass for privacy and light control

Remember the details

Contemporary style is in the details—albeit a few sleek, carefully selected ones. Include these items in your bath design for a clean, modern aesthetic:

- Simple metal knobs and pulls
- Nature-inspired tiles in warm earthtones
- Clutter-free countertops, maybe one or two favorite items for ornamentation
- Sculptural fixtures such as raised-granite lavatory bowls and stainless-steel faucets
- Light fixtures with contemporary shades for directed light
- Walls adorned with neutral hues, natural tiles, or textural wallcoverings such as grass cloth

A tiny powder room is big on style with green walls, a concrete sink on mahogany legs, and stylized lighting. Niches cut into the wall provide clutter-free display space.

A 7-inch-deep knee wall covered in black granite contains plumbing hookups while providing a ledge for stacking towels and displaying art behind a sleek white tub.

Whirlpool Tub or Soaking Tub?

Many new contemporary-style bathrooms feature soaking tubs rather than whirlpools. The opportunity to soothe sore muscles or frazzled nerves in a bubbling tub is definitely appealing, but will you take the time to do it? Keep in mind that large whirlpool tubs take a long time to fill, are often noisy, and may require additional structural support because they are extremely heavy when filled. You may also need a larger (or second) hot water heater to fill the tub while servicing the hot water to other rooms in the house. If a whirlpool is a must-have in your new bath, make sure you insulate the room for sound or spend the extra money for a quieter model.

With sunny walls, golden iridescent tiles, and clear glass vessel sinks, this bath shows that contemporary can be warm and welcoming.

DESIGN GALLERY
Contemporary Details

To establish a contemporary retreat—whether it's sleek and stylish, colorful and fun, or tranquil and soothing—look to these modern interpretations for inspiration.

1. For contemporary style with energy, choose graphic patterns. Mod-style wallpaper and long narrow tiles installed vertically on the tub surround do the trick.

2. Bold color and texture are the rule here. A satinized glass sink, orange walls, blue glass tiles, polished-chrome fittings, and stainless steel make the most of clean-line style.

3. A custom concrete trough sink takes a minimalist approach while maximizing space.

4. Stained oak doors provide a stunning entrance to a sophisticated, serene bath.

5. A bronze basin, angled limestone countertop, and grass-cloth wallcovering blend function with Asian-inspired serenity.

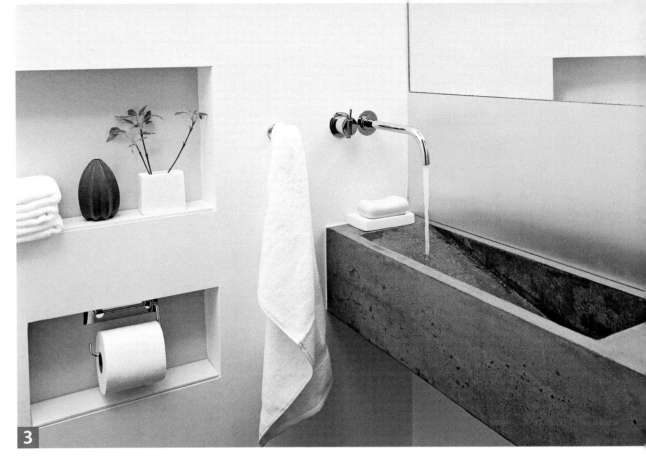

FRESH COUNTRY STYLE

The elements of fresh country style include natural materials; handmade items blessed with imperfections; and a nostalgic selection of fabrics, colors, and forms. A few touches of country style go a long way toward warming cold floors and easy-clean counters. Country style takes many forms, from the rich colors and old-fashioned fabrics of true-blue country to the pastel shades and delicate accents of a cottage look. Choose your favorite style within this genre, and you'll find endless ways to make your bath a venue for personal expression.

Include common elements

Although the many interpretations of country style have their own eclectic touches, you're likely to find some of these elements in most country-style baths:

- White-painted cabinetry paired with wood flooring, new wood distressed to look old, or raw planks
- Living room comfort in the form of upholstered chairs, padded window seats, throw pillows, and flowing fabric valances
- Charming, mismatched furnishings—perhaps an old pine wardrobe as a storage cabinet or an heirloom dresser converted to a vanity
- Vintage-look fixtures including freestanding tubs, pedestal sinks, and old-fashioned faucets

Pedestal sinks, freestanding cabinetry, and arborlike columns pair with garden-print wallpaper and beaded-board wainscoting. The result: a bath that blends classic farmhouse style with the architecture of an outdoor room.

Both functional and unique, the country accessories here inject flavor in the bath. To achieve a fresh country style in your bath, display favorite items on a rustic shelf and drape a curtain around a clawfoot tub.

Remember the details

This is where country decorating gets fun. The details you select will determine the country style your bath possesses. Mix and match these elements for your own interpretation:

- Vintage braided throw rugs
- Wallpaper or beaded board on the walls
- Wicker baskets as hampers and storage containers
- Groupings of antique glass jars holding bath salts or cotton balls
- Windows adorned with airy lace or sheers
- Accessories, including plates, old hats, interesting frames, and seashells
- Antique chandeliers or collectibles transformed into lighting fixtures
- A variety of prints: florals, stripes, checks, and plaids
- Rustic, rough-hewn furniture
- Vintage-look or salvaged faucets, doorknobs, and other hardware

Design Tip

Today's fresh country look is sparer than it was 30 years ago. Pick a unifying element—whether it's a color, pattern, material, or shape—to fill your bath with your favorite vintage items without overwhelming the space.

Cottage style doesn't have to cost a fortune when affordable beaded-board wainscoting, a yellow and white palette, and well-placed flowers steal the show.

Colors of the sea and shore, along with beachy accessories, enliven this freestanding tub—the focal point of a bath with rustic charm.

DESIGN GALLERY
Fresh Country Details

Country style is a look loved for its ties to the past. Fresh country, with its updated attitude, achieves modern popularity with simpler shapes, bolder patterns, fresher colors, and less clutter.

1. Carry out the vintage look with a tub filler complete with a handheld shower.

2. A charming anteroom with vine-pattern wallpaper signals the garden-inspired atmosphere of a master bath retreat.

3. A pie safe or stand-alone cupboard is perfect for storing towels and toiletries in a country bathroom.

4. Shuttered casement windows above the tub and cream beaded-board wainscoting nod to country style.

5. An antique handpainted basin, part of a porcelain collection, works double duty as a functional fixture.

French style is in the details of this dressy vanity area, where antique mirrors and light fixtures from France hang above built-in cabinetry with Sheraton-style legs and central drawers.

WORLD STYLE

As a decorative theme, world style avoids strict definition. The form it takes depends on which country (or countries) you choose to re-create in your bathroom retreat. Perhaps you've found inspiration in the elegance of a European hotel, the character of a Spanish villa, antique artifacts from the Far East, or the clean lines of Japanese style.

The influences of world style span time as well as the globe, allowing you to draw on an eclectic collection of elements borrowed from several periods. You may include details culled from your family's ethnic backgrounds, a passion for history, or a specific geographic area. Although many influences may come into play in your bathroom, only two of the most common are addressed here.

Old-world influences

In decorating, old world typically refers to inspiration from the European continent. Although the styles of many countries or regions are distinctive, certain commonalities flourish in their American bathroom translations.

If old-world style is your taste, remember that successful design relies on a degree of authenticity. This is not a genre of built-in cabinets or standard-issue fixtures. Rather you might find plastered walls, unmatched furnishings with hand-glazed treatments, and elaborate moldings. Ornate fixtures, luxurious materials, and a sense of history abound.

Design Tip

One of the keys to successfully mixing styles, eras, and world influences is scale. Distinctive pieces coexist peacefully when their scale is common to the overall design at work.

Custom craftsmanship and layering of materials lend an old-world feel to new cabinetry. Copper insets grace the cherry doors. The stone floor echoes that of cathedrals and sculpture.

Treat the bathroom walls as you would those in the living room and finish them with elegant coverings, special faux paint treatments, or woodwork. Look for antique and reproduction furnishings that suit a formal space. Intricate carvings and elegant, graceful details are common on everything from chairs to furniture-style vanities. Lovely lighting is present too in the form of crystal chandeliers, ornate sconces, and reproduction fixtures. Also look for artwork or mirrors in lavish gilt frames, decorative boxes with silver plating, antique or reproduction rugs, brass fixtures, and other treasures discovered at antique stores and flea markets or during world travels.

Asian inspiration

With the right design and decor, a household bathroom can channel the ambience and spirit of an Asian spa. Zen principles are based on spiritual stillness and harmony

Far Eastern influences show their practical side in this bath. A retrofit 100-year-old Indonesian ceramic vessel serves as a sink, and toiletries tuck into an antique Indian cabinet next to the tub. The stone tile brings a feeling of the outdoors.

through visual balance; these concepts easily translate into the restrained details and minimal ornamentation in baths.

Earthy materials possess an aura of quiet reflection. Cool colors and gentle lighting help soothe stressed minds and soften the edges of dark stone. Aside from Zen principles, other Asian influences include shoji screens, lantern-style sconces, and natural materials and colors. Look for neutral hues such as black, white, and soft gray, which pair with warmer neutrals like cream, taupe, and brown. Plan sufficient storage so the minimalist decor takes precedence. Plain-front cabinets crafted from fine-grain and exotic woods (think teak, bird's-eye maple, and black walnut) fit in beautifully.

This bath, based on the flavors of southern Europe, combines rustic antiquity with Mediterranean serenity. Brightly colored handcrafted tiles set in cement-color grout line the bathing area; open French windows usher in breezes.

DESIGN GALLERY
World Style Influences

Design ideas come from many places: memories of a childhood home, vacation destinations, or treasured objects, to name a few. Travel the globe (mentally or physically) to discover the details that best personalize your worldly space.

1. This bath shows off its reverence for old world-style with Venetian plaster walls, dark woods, and a custom-weave rug over walnut-plank flooring.

2. An antique tub with an unexpected exterior of polished nickel sets the tone in this bath of many mirrors.

3. Mosaic tiles bring to mind the glamour of the Italian Renaissance.

4. Muted light shining through shoji screens makes the room glow, a perfect backdrop for a long soak in a Japanese tub.

5. A 19th-century beach screen, crystal candelabra, and mirrored chandelier introduce a sense of decadent luxury to this Italian-inspired bath.

6. A pagoda-style vanity of limestone and mahogany exemplifies the restrained style of Asia.

Plan the plumbing layout early in the process to determine the ideal placement for showers and other bathroom fixtures.

CHAPTER 3

Bath Design Basics

Plumbing Basics, Numbers to Know,
Small-Bath Solutions, Universal Design,
Privacy, Safety, Green Building

Follow established recommendations for clearances around common bathroom elements including tubs and vanities to ensure easy access for everyone in the family.

At this point in the design process you've undertaken the basics of planning your bath remodel, envisioned your dream bath, and identified your personal style. Now it's time to get into the plumbing configuration and layout for your bathroom.

You'll find a rundown of common plumbing layouts and how they affect your bath design in this chapter. The recommended clearances around bathroom fixtures play a significant role in creating your floor plan and ensuring comfort once your bathroom is complete. Privacy, safety, and the incorporation of universal design elements are considerations too. If you're designing a small bath, see pages 78–79 for ways to fit the necessities—and some extras—into a small footprint. Green building is more than a fad, so you'll want to consider smart products that can help you save energy, money, and the environment. It all adds up to moving another step closer to a bath that's easy on the eyes and the body.

PLUMBING BASICS

The layout of your bathroom fixtures affects your plumbing bill. The fewer "wet walls" you have, the less costly your plumbing installation will be. When remodeling take maximum advantage of your present plumbing. Replacing old fixtures with new ones in the same location is fairly simple. Installing new plumbing runs (called roughing in) to place fixtures in new locations requires skill and planning. It may also require a plumbing license, so check with your building department before doing work yourself. In any case when planning to add bathroom fixtures, place them as close as possible to existing plumbing to keep new runs short. If you don't, costs can skyrocket.

In general a home plumbing system consists of two networks of pipes. One is the supply system—the pipes that carry water into the house and distribute it to your plumbing fixtures. The other plumbing network is the drain, waste, and vent (DWV) system, which carries drain water, waste, and harmful gases out of the house.

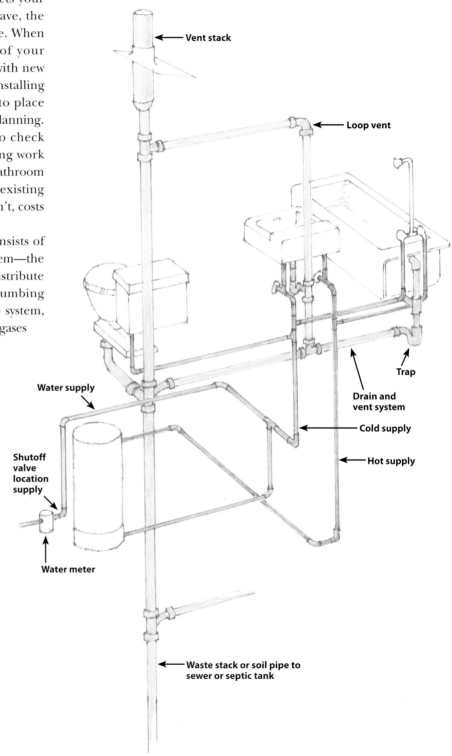

Vent stack

Loop vent

Trap

Water supply

Drain and vent system

Cold supply

Hot supply

Shutoff valve location supply

Water meter

Waste stack or soil pipe to sewer or septic tank

Supply, Drain, Waste, and Vent Systems

The supply system brings water into the house, divides it into hot and cold water lines, and distributes it to fixtures. The drain system carries water away from fixtures and out of the house. The vent system supplies air to the drainpipes so waste flows out freely.

Wet Wall Options

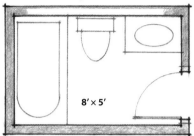

8' × 5'

One-wall layout. A design with all the supply and draining pipes located within one wall is more cost efficient but limits your design possibilities. You may want to consider this layout if you are creating a new bath space and have to supply water to the area.

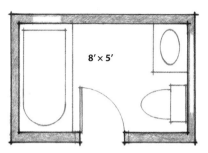

8' × 5'

Two-wall layout. A design with plumbing in two walls requires more plumbing work but offers more floor area and storage space around the sink.

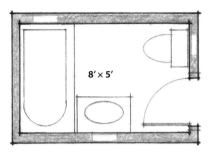

8' × 5'

Three-wall layout. Three-wall layouts offer the most design flexibility, but they require more space and more complex plumbing.

Supply

In the supply system an underground line from a water source connects to a meter that measures the amount of water entering the house. Next to the meter is a shutoff valve that, when closed, stops water from flowing into the house. The main supply line branches into two lines—one for cold water and one for hot. The cold-water supply line feeds the network of supply pipes throughout the house. The hot-water supply line goes to your water heater. From there the hot-water pipes run parallel with the cold-water pipes to serve various fixtures and faucets.

Your home's water-supply system is pressurized, but the drain-waste system depends on gravity. These pipes also are connected to vents, which allow sewer gases to escape harmlessly up a chimneylike vent stack. Plumbing vents also allow the entire DWV system to maintain atmospheric pressure so the flow of wastewater is not affected by vacuums, back-pressure, or siphoning.

Design Tip

Beyond the fixtures themselves one of the most expensive aspects of a bath upgrade involves moving plumbing lines. If you are renovating or enlarging, consider whether it's possible to leave water pipes and drains in the same place.

Drains and vents

Because each new or moved bathroom fixture must connect with a main soil stack, you must know the locations of your main vents, then determine a route for attaching new vent lines to them. You may live in an area where building codes specify the size and general conformation of drainage, waste, and vent lines. Once again consult local codes and hire a licensed professional plumber if necessary. Unless you're an accomplished do-it-yourselfer, it's best to leave major plumbing jobs to a professional.

Rerouting plumbing is a much easier job if the house has a basement or crawlspace. If the house is built on a concrete slab, adding new baths or fixtures may require demolishing part of the slab to gain access to main plumbing lines. Also check to see whether your water heater has enough capacity to meet the added hot-water demand. You may want to add another water heater.

Plumbing layouts

When placing fixtures in your bathroom, think about how they are used and in which order. The sink, for example, should be positioned closest to the door because it's often the only fixture used or the last stop in most people's bathing routines. The tub and shower can be farthest from the door because they are not used as frequently. Your bathroom plumbing layout probably will fall into one of the three categories shown above.

Console sinks are particularly user friendly because they provide knee space beneath the countertop. To prevent burns, set exposed pipes as far back as possible.

Design Tip

When you're calculating how much space fixtures, cabinetry, and other common bathroom elements occupy, you may want to include room for amenities such as a seating area, dressing room, or breakfast bar. Many bathrooms today include more than the basics, and now is the time to reconsider all the extras you put on your bathroom remodeling list.

This bath's generous size provides plenty of elbow room between each task area.

NUMBERS TO KNOW

Based on average space measurements and needs, professional designers have developed recommendations for minimum clearance around doors, fixtures, cabinets, and other common bathroom elements. The following guidelines that the National Kitchen and Bath Association (NKBA) outlined are meant to work well for anyone at any stage in life, although some of these dimensions are smaller than the accessible design recommendations described on pages 80–83. Keep in mind that these are just recommended minimums. Allow more space if the fit is too tight for any intended users.

Floor space guidelines

Universal design standards recommend leaving at least 30×48 inches of clear floor space in front of each fixture. Clear floor spaces suggested at each fixture may overlap. You can add the clear space between a toilet and a tub together; make sure that the amount of space between the two meets the minimum guidelines for each.

Door openings. Doorways should be at least 32 inches wide. Allow clear floor space at least the width of the door on the push side and a larger clear floor space on the pull side to allow room for users to comfortably open and close the door and pass through the doorway.

Walkways. Make passages between the bathroom walls and fixtures at least 36 inches wide.

Sink fronts. Allow at least 30 inches of clear floor space in front of each sink. To meet the universal design standard of 30×48 inches, up to 12 of the 48 inches can extend beneath the sink if there is open knee space there.

Toilet allowance. Leave a clear floor space of 30 inches in front of the toilet. Leave at least 16 inches of space from the centerline of the fixture to the closest fixture or sidewall. If you install a toilet in a separate compartment, make the compartment at least 36 inches wide and 66 inches long. Install a swing-out door or a pocket door on the opening to the compartment. The doorway should be at least 32 inches wide.

Bidet allowance. Leave a clear floor space of 30 inches in front of the bidet. Allow at least 18 inches from the centerline of the fixture to the closest fixture or sidewall. When the toilet and bidet are side by side, maintain the 18 inches minimum clearance to all obstructions. Follow toilet allowance guidelines for a bidet/toilet combination.

Bathtub entrance. Plan a 30-inch section of clear space adjacent to the length of the tub if you'll approach the fixture from the side.

Shower entrance. For showers less than 60 inches wide, plan a clear floor space that is 36 inches deep and 12 inches wider than the shower. For wider showers plan for a clear floor space that is 36 inches deep and as wide as the shower.

Shower interior. The recommended minimum usable interior dimensions, measured from wall to wall, are 36×36 inches, but some people prefer more room. If there isn't enough space, you can reduce this to 32×32 inches, but it will result in a cramped fit for many users. Design the shower doors so they can open into the bathroom—not into the stall—to avoid crowding the space in the shower.

Shower and tub controls. Position controls so you can reach them from inside and outside the shower and tub.

Gain More Room

If the available space in your home is so tight that it prevents you from following some of the NKBA floor space recommendations, first consider whether a bumpout or addition is an option. If not, try these strategies:

Eliminate interior walls and partitions. Even though nonload-bearing walls within the bathroom are ideal for creating privacy, they take up precious floor space.

Select smaller fixtures. An extensive range of styles, shapes, and sizes is available for virtually every bath fixture.

Revise your requirements. If your bath wish list includes a separate tub and shower or an oversize whirlpool tub, think about what you most need and want. Rather than trying to cram everything in, go with the essentials.

Grooming space guidelines

These NKBA guidelines ensure that everyone in the bath has adequate grooming space and elbowroom near the sink, vanities, and countertops.

Sink space. Leave at least 15 inches clearance from the centerline of a sink to the closest sidewall. If you are including two sinks in a vanity, leave at least 30 inches clearance between the centerlines of each. If the sinks are wider than 30 inches, increase the distance by several inches to provide a minimum of 8 inches of open counterspace between them. Taking such measures ensures adequate elbowroom when both sinks are in use.

Vanity height. If you are including two vanities, consider positioning them at different heights—32 to 43 inches—to match the comfort level of the people who use them. Vanity cabinets are typically 30 to 32 inches high, while kitchen base cabinets are typically 36 inches high. Many people find the 36-inch height more comfortable for standing. If space allows add a 30-inch-high section with knee space below for sitting.

Mirror height. Locate a vanity mirror at eye level for the primary users. Or if you like, position it higher above the floor and tilt the top of the mirror away from the wall.

Door and drawer widths. When designing a vanity cabinet, split doors in cabinets that are 24 inches or wider. Large single doors can be awkward to open, especially in a narrow bathroom. Avoid narrow doors and drawers. Nine-inch widths generally are too narrow.

Corner comfort. To eliminate sharp corners, order countertops with rounded corners and eased edges.

Leaving at least 15 inches clearance from the centerline of a sink to the closest sidewall allows users plenty of space for hand and face washing.

It may be difficult to follow all of the recommended space guidelines in a small bath. Although the bench shown intrudes on the recommended clear floor space in front of the tub, it's a useful spot for storing towels within reach and drying off after a bath.

SMALL BATH SOLUTIONS

Would you like to make your bath look, feel, and live larger without major renovation? The key is to keep the overall design simple so the bath seems open and inviting rather than cramped.

Smaller scale bathroom fixtures preserve precious inches when a floor plan is tight. For instance wall-hung toilets take up considerably less space than standard models—plus they're easier to clean. If you can do without a bath, opt for a walk-in shower rather than a tub-shower combination. Glass shower walls create the illusion of spaciousness.

To increase floor space even more, consider replacing a standard-size vanity with a smaller or custom version. Pedestal or wallmount sinks take up even less room, but you'll sacrifice storage. Make up for the lost undercounter space by installing a wall-hung medicine cabinet in place of a standard vanity mirror. You can also build a ledge that's wide enough for stashing other toiletries behind the sink.

Beyond the basics

The same design principles that make other areas of your home seem larger can enhance the sense of space in your bathroom. Use these tips.

Use neutral hues. Pastels, whites, and other soft colors that reflect light help a room seem larger. To visually expand the space even more, paint the ceiling a lighter hue than the walls or make the trim disappear by painting it to match the wall color. Save darker colors for accents.

Go with the flow. Echo the color scheme used in an adjacent room. When your space is small, it helps to borrow colors and styles from nearby rooms. Keeping the flow continuous makes both rooms feel larger.

Accentuate the horizontal. Elements such as vanity tops, single shelves, and painted or tiled stripes play tricks that make a space seem wider.

Look to the ceiling. No way to physically expand your space? Fool the eye by emphasizing the room's height with tile, a wallpaper border, or interesting ceiling treatments.

Lighten up. Windows let in light, fresh air, and scenic views while preventing small baths from feeling cramped and claustrophobic. If your bath is on an exterior wall, install or increase the size of the windows. At the very least emphasize what you have by minimizing the use of shades and other window treatments.

Use mirrors. In addition to reflecting light throughout the room, horizontal mirrors perceptibly double the size of your space. Save vertical floor-to-ceiling mirrors for your bedroom or dressing room.

Careful planning made possible a roomy whirlpool tub and walk-in shower in this small bath. A glass block partition hides the toilet from view without blocking light. A see-through shower door visually opens the space.

An egg-shape toilet and rounded wallmount sink eliminate sharp edges in tight quarters.

Although this bath is tiny, it's loaded with character thanks to embossed silver-painted wallpaper and a vanity built from salvaged beaded board.

UNIVERSAL DESIGN

The goal of universal design is to make all users as independent and comfortable as possible. Even if no one has special needs now, planning a bath that can accommodate family and guests regardless of age or physical ability enhances the long-term livability and enjoyment of your home.

If you're building a new home, you can incorporate universal design principles from the get-go. If you are planning an accessible bath for an existing home, you'll probably need to borrow square footage from surrounding spaces to make room for necessary improvements.

Easy-access ideas
Incorporating these accessible options ensures your bath will be comfortable, attractive, and usable for years to come.

Elegant yet practical grab bars make it easy to move around this semiprivate toilet area. DaVinci-inspired sketches on the wall are a decorative touch.

Location, location, location. A practical barrier-free bath starts with the room's location. It should be situated on the ground floor so there are no stairs to climb.

Door size. Plan for a clear door opening of at least 34 inches. Openings larger than 38 inches make it difficult to open and close doors from a seated position; narrower openings make it difficult, if not impossible, for a wheelchair to get through.

Handle selection. Equip entrance doors, drawers, and faucets with lever or D-shape handles. They are easier to operate than knobs, especially for young children and people with arthritis or limited mobility.

Floor space. A typical-size wheelchair can make a turnaround in a 5-foot-diameter area of clear floor space. Leave an area in front of the sink that measures at least 30×48 inches (although the clear floor space can overlap with other fixtures). Provide 48 square inches of clear floor space for the toilet and 60×60 inches in front of the tub.

Shower stalls. Shower stalls are easier to get into and out of than bathtubs. Choose a stall with no curb or a very short one. Slope the floor toward the drain to ensure the water stays within the enclosure. Shower stalls must measure at least 4 feet square with an opening that is at least 36 inches wide. Include grab bars, a single-handle lever control, a handheld shower spray, and a built-in bench or seat that is 17 to 19 inches high.

Bathtubs. If a tub is a necessity, install grab bars in the tub along the sidewall and the two end walls. Install the bars 33 to 36 inches above the floor and another set 9 inches above the tub rim. The bars must be at least 24 inches long. Avoid installing steps for climbing into the tub. They too easily become slippery in a wet environment.

Shower and bath controls. Design shower and bath surrounds so you can reach the controls from inside and outside the stall. Put the controls 38 to 48 inches above the floor and above a grab bar if there is one. For a handheld showerhead model, locate the head no higher than 48 inches above the floor when in its lowest position.

Knee space. The knee space under a sink should be about 27 inches high and 30 inches wide. In addition insulate or conceal hot water pipes to protect users from burns.

There's no slippery shower threshold to worry about with a barrier-free shower. This one includes fixed and handheld showerheads for ease of use.

Rounded countertop edges, open space under the sink, and a single-handle faucet combine to create a vanity area that's beautiful and accessible. The surrounding drawers and cabinets are easy to reach from a seated position.

Toilets. The ideal placement for a toilet is in a corner of the bath so you can install grab bars behind the toilet and next to it. Leave at least 48 inches of clear floor space to one side or in front of the toilet. A toilet 3 inches higher than a conventional model makes it easier to transfer to or from a wheelchair. As a general rule, grab bars near the toilet are 33 to 36 inches above the floor. They are 42 inches long on a sidewall and not more than 12 inches from the back wall. The bar on the back wall must be at least 23 inches long and extend at least 12 inches from each side of the center of the toilet.

Grab bars. Rated to withstand up to 300 pounds of pressure, grab bars are helpful only if they are attached securely. Fasten them to wall studs. If possible, before putting up drywall, install ¾-inch plywood sheathing over the studs from floor to ceiling. You can then install bars anywhere on the walls as needed. Buy bars with a nonslip texture. They come in a variety of colors and styles.

Lighting. In addition to general lighting, provide task lighting for each functional area of the bathroom. Include at least one light that's controlled by a wall switch, with the switch placed 3 feet 6 inches above the floor at the entrance to the bathroom. Paddle switches are the easiest to use.

Mirrors. Hang mirrors above sinks with the bottom edge of their reflecting surfaces no more than 40 inches above the floor. Mirrors that tilt accommodate seated or standing users.

Windows. Casement windows are the easiest to operate from a wheelchair. Install them 24 to 30 inches above the floor so that wheelchair users can open, close, and easily see out of them.

Storage. Plan storage of frequently used items 15 to 48 inches above the floor. Broad, shallow shelves put items within easy reach of someone seated. Equip cabinetry with roll-out wire bins or shelves for easier access. Moveable furniture and open shelves are best.

Design Tip

For more information about universal design, contact the Center for Universal Design at 800/647-6777 or visit design .ncsu.edu/cud. To purchase a copy of the National Kitchen and Bath Association's planning guidelines that include access standards, call 800/843-6522 or visit nkba.org.

Limestone tiles distinguish the bath area from the sleep area in this master suite. Flooring with low or no thresholds makes for safe, easy transitions between rooms.

PRIVACY

The bathroom by its very nature is a private sanctuary. To allow multiple family members to use the bathroom at the same time, you may wish to install pocket doors between the major functional areas. Compartmentalizing a master bath enables two people to share the bathroom while offering privacy to each. Separate compartments typically house the toilet (and sometimes include a bidet and a shower). As a design compromise, a half-wall offers modest separation between portions of the bath without completely closing off sections of the room from one another.

Where you reside also has an effect on how much privacy you need. If you live in a secluded area, window coverings may be less of an issue than in the city where a neighbor's window may be only a few feet away. Likewise narrow horizontal windows placed high on the wall work well in a second-story suburban bath, but when placed on the first floor, they often put the bath within view of a neighbor's second floor.

Frosted or stained-glass windows provide privacy without blocking all of the light. Glass block admits light while obscuring views. Some blocks distort views and conserve heat better than others; choose a style that works for you. Avoid thick, heavy window treatments that will soak up moisture. Quick-drying cotton works well, although you may need to line the curtains to avoid transparency. Moisture-resistant fabrics designed for outdoor use are available in a variety of colors and patterns. Venetian blinds, vertical blinds, miniblinds, and pull-down shades also work well while enabling you to control the amount of light.

A separate toilet room, above, provides maximum seclusion. Transoms above the door allow more light into the room. A frosted-glass compartment, below, separates the toilet and shower from the rest of the bath without blocking light.

Design Tip

Like visual privacy, acoustic privacy is also a concern in bathroom design. A ventilating fan can serve as white noise, drowning out the sound of a flushing toilet. Insulating the bathroom walls also helps. Look in home centers for wallboard designed to deaden sound.

SAFETY

The accessible design guidelines on pages 80–83 are designed with safety in mind, but other factors also increase safety in the bathroom.

- **GFCI outlets.** Protect all receptacles, lights, and switches in the room with ground fault circuit interrupters (GFCIs) to reduce the risk of electrical shocks. Install only moistureproof light fixtures above the tub and shower areas. Power cords stretched over a counter are dangerous so be sure each vanity area has its own power supply.

- **Flooring.** Flooring, such as polished stone or smooth hardwood, is especially slippery when wet so choose varieties with naturally nonslip textures or plan to include skidproof mats around areas that are likely to get wet. Add rubber footpads to step stools and vanity chairs to help keep them from slipping out from under you when you're using them.

- **Surfaces.** To avoid cuts and bruises add a waterproof cushion to the tub spout. If possible select countertops and cabinetry with rounded corners.

- **Latches.** Install a childproof latch on the toilet and childproof locks on the cabinets if you have children in your house.

- **Water.** Turn your hot water heater down to 120 degrees. Or install a pressure-balancing/temperature regulator or a temperature-limiting device for faucet heads, particularly showerheads, to prevent scalding. To prevent drowning never leave a child unattended in the tub.

A telephone installed in an easy-to-reach spot in the bathroom is a smart amenity. Then users can call for help if necessary.

GREEN BUILDING

The process of green building is growing more popular—and for good reason. Green building works to minimize the environmental impact of construction by incorporating environmental considerations into the home building process. It encompasses everything from lot selection to the choice of materials. The reason? According to the National Association of Home Builders, resource-efficient design and development practices reduce the environmental impact of construction, optimize renewable resources, and improve the energy performance of housing, which means your home will be less expensive to operate and more comfortable to live in.

Better bath, better environment

Even if your remodeling plans include only your existing bathroom, the selection of energy-efficient fixtures and green building materials can greatly benefit your quality of life and pocketbook (as well as the environment) in the long run. Whenever possible use salvaged or recycled-content building materials and locally available indigenous materials. Beyond these recommendations consider:

Low-flow fixtures. These fixtures are designed to do the job as well as their standard counterparts while using considerably less water. The most efficient ultralow-flow toilets use less than 1.6 gallons per minute (gpm) of water per flush. Water-efficient showerheads with a flow rate of less than 2.6 gpm and sink faucets that use less than 2.2 gpm are also recommended.

Countertops. Choose from a variety of environmentally friendly countertop materials. Highly durable sustainable surfacing is made from recycled glass and concrete; it's as strong as granite and less porous than marble. Natural quartz surfacing is good for countertops, tub and shower surrounds, and backsplashes. It resists scratching, comes with built-in antimicrobial protection, and is certified safe for use because it has low-to-no off-gassing.

Flooring. Try natural cork, which is sustainably forested, chemical free, and hypoallergenic. Reclaimed wood, bamboo, and recycled glass tile are other options.

Wood products. Use wood materials that are reclaimed or certified sustainable, such as bamboo, for cabinets and other materials in your bath. Make sure particleboard, medium-density fiberboard (MDF), and other manufactured materials are certified for low formaldehyde emissions.

Design Tip

Energy efficiency is a large component of green building. Buy Energy Star-rated fixtures, lighting (compact fluorescent lights are the way to go), windows, and ventilation systems to ensure your new bath will be less expensive to operate and more comfortable to spend time in.

This modern bathroom floor is made of bamboo, an environmentally friendly material. Many people opt for bamboo because it requires no pesticides and takes only a few years to reach maturity.

Natural slate tiles and cabinets of blackened steel salvaged from scrap yards lend an earthy aesthetic to this modern bath.

Low- or no-VOC paints. Paints, stains, and other architectural coatings produce volatile organic compounds (VOCs), which are an integral component of smog. Also VOCs can cause respiratory, skin, and eye irritation; headaches; nausea; and more serious health problems. The solution: Use low- or no-VOC sealants and paints (available in colors similar to standard paint brands) in your bathroom.

Ventilation. Install an Energy Star-rated fan, which provides more ventilation capacity at a lower wattage than a standard bath fan. You can control it with a timer or humidistat. It's best to run the fan for 20 minutes after baths or showers.

Why Go Green?

The National Association of Home Builders lists several benefits that owners of green homes have experienced:

Lower operating costs. Energy and water efficiency measures reduce utility bills.

Increased comfort. With fewer drafts and better humidity control, green homes are more comfortable year-round.

Improved environmental quality. Choosing materials with fewer chemicals, controlling moisture, and selecting efficient air and filtration systems contributes to a healthier indoor environment.

Less maintenance. Longer-lasting materials require fewer resources for replacement and reduce maintenance and repair costs.

DESIGN GALLERY
Accessible Baths

Designing a bath that everyone in your family can use now and for years to come is worth the extra planning and is fairly easy to achieve. As these details prove, universal design elements are beautiful things.

1. It's easy to adjust the height of the showerhead on this wall. The utilitarian look is part of its minimalist appeal.

2. A console sink provides legroom for seated users.

3. The tub's sturdy grab bars offer a helping hand. The handheld shower spray makes washing hair a cinch.

4. A sensor allows users to switch this faucet on and off—and control the temperature—without ever touching it.

5. Faucets that operate with a single lever are easiest to use.

As part of a bathroom renovation in a 1920s home, this vanity takes cues from the style of the time. The marble counter and rosewood cabinetry have period appeal.

CHAPTER 4

Plan the Project

Bath Facelifts, Renovate, Enlarge, Convert,
Plan an Addition, Floor Plans

Bath remodeling projects typically fall into at least one of five categories: a facelift involving cosmetic changes; a renovation that changes the layout within an existing bathroom; an expansion extending an existing bath into adjacent space; a conversion transforming existing square footage to bathroom use; and an addition that includes a brand new bathroom. The following pages illustrate what you can accomplish with each approach. Drafting a floor plan at this stage enables you to determine more precisely which approach to take.

A master bath with an open floor plan puts to use spacesaving shoji screens with sliding panels. When closed the panels become a wall, creating two private, cozy rooms.

BATH FACELIFTS

If you're faced with a bath that works well but suffers from dated colors or worn fixtures, a facelift may provide the right fix, typically at a budget-friendly price. Facelifts include nonstructural cosmetic changes, such as repainting the walls, resurfacing the walls or tub surround, and/or replacing fixtures, flooring, and countertops. Simple applications of tile or even a fresh coat of paint and new hardware can work magic, transforming a bland space into a beautiful room.

Though such cosmetic changes typically cost far less than any other type of bath project, it's important to plan a facelift as carefully as you would a complete renovation. Start by consulting the list you made of what you like and dislike about the bathroom. If the problems are cosmetic, a facelift should serve well. If, however, the real problems lie in a lack of space, misplaced fixtures, or poor layout, a new coat of paint obviously won't address the issues. In such a case it's worth determining if a couple of inexpensive quick fixes will make you happier until you can address the real problems. If not, look ahead to the sections on renovations, conversions, and additions in this chapter. If so, check out these ideas for maximum-impact, minimum-budget solutions:

Visual-enhancement strategies

If the bathroom appears too small even when it's adequately sized to serve its purpose, implement fool-the-eye techniques to visually enlarge it. Install a large wall mirror that stretches the space by reproducing its image. Glass shower doors let the eye see through a solid surface, opening the room instead of chopping it into small blocks.

Make storage count

As you upgrade your bathroom, make an effort to maintain storage space without sacrificing charm. Get more storage and function from existing cabinets by catering to specific storage needs. Bins, baskets, and roll-out storage trays create space customized for bath essentials. Consider using freestanding furniture to supplement storage.

Impact with color

You can freshen a dated bathroom with color. Start with a favorite color, then select one or two complementary colors as accents. Apply the main color to the walls and accessorize with towels, throw rugs, and window treatments in accent colors. If your favorite color is too bold for the walls, you may want to select a more neutral hue and sprinkle one or two vibrant favorites throughout the bath. For more information about color, see pages 42–45.

Increase the light

The right light fixtures in the right locations make grooming easier. If lighting is a problem, add another fixture or two. Replace heavy window treatments with sheers that ensure privacy but admit light and offer a sense of the view beyond.

A new countertop and sink can breathe new life into a bath. This frosted-glass vessel sink intersects the countertop's matching glass tile accents.

Cosmetic enhancements revive the bathroom in a 75-year-old Mediterranean-style house. Honey-tinted walls accented with white woodwork freshen the mood.

DESIGN GALLERY
Style Enhancements

Opportunities for enhancing the look of your bathroom are limited only by your imagination. Attention to detail, as shown here, results in a rejuvenating wake-up for even the most tired bath.

1. Affordable beaded-board wainscoting, inexpensive white fixtures, and standard white field tile bring to life this once-dark bathroom.

2. Coordinating tub and sink faucets, cabinetry hardware, and a chandelier instantly refresh this period-style bath.

3. This oil-rubbed bronze tub faucet and handle set will develop a patina over time. The simplistic style is Asian-inspired.

4. Shapely cabinetry pulls made of solid bronze with a brushed-nickel finish make for hand-friendly and visually appealing hardware.

5. The simple neutral tile surround complements a bold yet serene work of art.

RENOVATE

When the overall size of your bathroom is adequate but not much else in the room functions as you want it to, renovation is likely the best solution. Renovation goes beyond cosmetic changes to more comprehensive jobs such as replacing fixtures, changing the layout, adding lighting, enlarging or replacing windows, and making structural changes short of expansion. Although this remodeling option is typically more costly than a facelift, it can dramatically change the functionality of your bath, possibly make it feel bigger, and give fixtures more room without adding on. With a full-scale renovation your bathroom will be out of service for a time. Careful planning is critical to minimize disruptions.

Relocate walls

Sometimes it's the floor plan rather than the overall dimensions that keeps a bath from functioning well. Renovating may require removing or adding walls within the existing bath space. The planning stage is the best time to imagine your bathroom with a different interior wall structure. Use the grid paper on page 205 to sketch the outer walls of the bathroom. Then experiment with a variety of configurations within that space until you develop the best solution to address your needs. Often reconfiguring walls within a bathroom is the key to a space that functions better and even feels more luxurious.

The goal for the master bathroom renovation shown here involved opening up a chopped space to create a room that appears remarkably larger than it is. Dividing walls were removed. A linen closet transformed into a glass-walled corner shower and open tub area. The sauna and toilet compartment became a closet. Room was opened up for a sit-down vanity in front of a window. Pullout towel storage between the makeup area and the sinks provides space-efficient storage.

Once necessary changes to the floor plan are made, look to the bath's remaining free space for instilling finer touches. In this bath bow-front cabinets and oval sinks take up scarcely more room than conventional ones but offer high-impact style. Gently sweeping satin-nickel pulls mimic the curve of sconces mounted high above the vanities.

Design Tip

If you find that the configuration of the bathroom hampers your plans, consider enlisting the help of a design professional. Designers, architects, and design-build firms are practiced at coming up with creative solutions to solve space and configuration dilemmas. See pages 188–189 for more information about professionals.

The round window above the double vanity supplied the inspiration for this master bath renovation. Oval sinks and bow-front cabinets create symmetry and further the curvaceous theme.

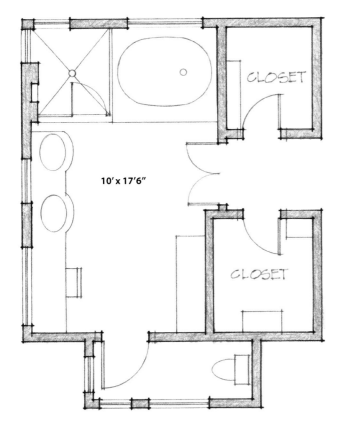

CLOSET

10' x 17'6"

CLOSET

Removing a wall made room for a sit-down makeup area in front of a window. A water-resistant finish protects the cherry counters throughout the bath.

Natural light plays an important role, funneling in through a picture window over the tub and a window in the clear-glass shower enclosure.

Go with the flow

Sometimes a few simple shifts make a room more functional. A new entry from the bedroom replaced the old, less-convenient entrance through an adjoining walk-in closet. A spacesaving pocket door installed for the closet freed additional floor space within the bath. The new freestanding tub positioned in the center of the room made space for a large shower enclosure that features multiple body sprays.

When square footage is tight, look for spacesaving features. In this room, a screen (not shown)—rather than the conventional separate compartment—hides the toilet.

This stunning bath renovation proves that it's possible to retain the original character of a home in the throes of remodeling. The stained-glass windows are original to this home. Two pairs of the windows remain intact, while the rest of the room underwent complete reconfiguration.

Modern convenience melds with period styling. The vanity's back shelf is reminiscent of an antique washstand. Antique sconces frame a leaded-glass panel.

Radiant-Heat Flooring Systems

Stone and tile floors feel cold against bare feet, but you can take the chill off of them with a radiant heating system. Radiant energy works when the warmth from the radiant system comes in contact with a cooler surface, such as a tile floor. The heat is also transferred to the air that comes in contact with the floor.

Three types of radiant systems are available: those with water pipes, electric elements, or air channels within the panel. Water and electric systems are most common. Electric systems have the lowest up-front cost, but depending on the cost of electric utilities in your area, operating costs over time may surpass those incurred using a water system. Almost any utility can heat water, so work with the installer to determine the most cost-effective option. Like other heating systems a thermostat controls radiant heating. Floor system radiant panels typically are attached beneath a subfloor or embedded in a concrete floor. Most flooring materials are suitable for use with a radiant floor heating system, but it's best to determine the surface before the system is installed.

A freestanding tub in the middle of the room allows space for a large shower with multiple body sprays and a clear glass enclosure.

The depth of the walk-in shower eliminates the need for a door. Clear glass protects the vanity from spray.

ENLARGE

Sometimes the amount of space in an existing bathroom is insufficient, and borrowing square footage from adjoining areas, such as a closet, hallway, or bedroom, is required. Annexing space from an adjoining room is often the best solution to problems caused by too-tight dimensions.

If possible look first to closets and other spaces that adjoin your bathroom's plumbing wall—the wall that contains plumbing pipes. It's far less expensive to install fixtures when you can connect them to nearby plumbing lines. Likewise, nonload-bearing walls that have few or no utility lines are much easier and less costly to remove than load-bearing walls with utility lines. If no interior space is available, porches and breezeways are the next most cost-effective choices for gaining space.

This bathroom nearly doubled in size when the former bath merged with an adjacent walk-in closet. The new space afforded room for a spacious whirlpool for two as well as the walk-in shower deep enough to eliminate the need for a shower door. A toilet compartment enables two people to use the bath with privacy.

The absorption of an entry area between the former closet and bath gave enough space for a lengthy double vanity that stretches between the tub and shower. Cabinetry lines the walls to maximize floor space.

The marriage of an old bathroom and a large master closet provides room for a whirlpool and five large windows that deliver stunning views.

8' x 21'3"

The shower room and adjoining main room share a glass block window. A chair and side table provide a comfortable spot to enjoy a morning cup of coffee.

Maximize Comfort

When you're renovating or enlarging an existing bath it pays to make it as comfortable as possible.

Ventilate. Proper ventilation keeps your bath free of mildew and moisture damage. Install overhead fans and operable windows to let air in and moisture out. Choose a ventilating fan that exchanges all the air in the room eight times or more per hour.

Add convenience. Allow at least 24 inches of towel-bar space for each person. Plan a towel bar no farther than 6 inches from the tub or shower entrance. Find room for a seat that enables you to towel off and dress comfortably.

Plan door swings. Consider the direction of shower door and cabinet door swings. Improper planning can create everyday hassles.

Trade openness and privacy. Keep your new bath feeling comfortable but not crowded. Replace swinging doors with pocket ones to conserve floor space. Use wall-hung cabinets and freestanding furniture to increase storage.

Open shelving and a window seat anchor the bath's seating area. Tile set against the stained plank floor helps define the bath from the bedroom in the open floor plan.

Take a little, gain a lot

Annexing a small amount of space from an adjoining room may have a minimal effect on that room, but the change will make a major impact on a small bath's functionality.

Expanding a bath even minimally can allow for a complete renaissance in style. Open up your bathroom with a large window and create space for an oversize tub with a relaxing view. This bath annexed only the smallest of spaces by removing the wall between the old bathroom and the adjacent master bedroom. The result is a stunning combined space with a bath that feels luxuriously spacious and a comfortable sitting area shared by bath and bedroom.

Original beams in a 1720 home were left exposed for extra character. Modern-style bath fixtures with clean lines and sharp geometry juxtapose with the home's historical architecture.

CONVERT

If you can't find space to enlarge an existing bathroom, the next best option may be to convert an unused or underused room. To convert some of your home's existing square footage into a full bath with a tub, toilet, and sink, you'll need a space that measures at least 5×7 feet. If a shower stall is substituted for the tub, you can get by with 3×7 feet. A powder room requires at least 3×6 feet or 4 feet square. (For more information about space requirements, see pages 75–77.) The ultimate compliment for any bathroom is that if it were to lack fixtures, you would still want to relax there. Keep this goal in mind as you plan your conversion.

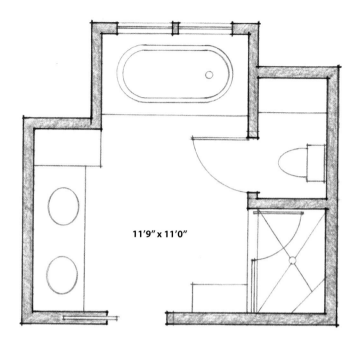

11'9" x 11'0"

Tucked into the dormer and under a window, the marble-encased tub couldn't be cozier.

A clear glass shower door showcases the shower's carrara marble walls and enhances the openness of the room.

Dramatic black-stained cabinetry was achieved through several steps. First the wood was stained black and then rubbed with steel wool to bring out the grain. Finally the surface was limed to highlight the grain.

Make a trade

When working within an existing space, take advantage of its limitations. In this bathroom a spacious tub nestles into a dormer alcove. A built-in unit to the left turns an otherwise unusable spot into functional storage. A vaulted ceiling sustains an illusion of spaciousness. Though the ceiling height in this bathroom is low in some places, the high peaks make the overall room feel expansive.

Design Tip

For the most convenient storage, think beyond the standard vanity and medicine cabinet. Take advantage of wall space by installing built-ins. Use the shallow space between walls for a niche that naturally accommodates small bath products.

Careful planning of this bath's interior preserved exterior features of the house including the size and location of this window. A raised edge along the back of the countertop keeps objects from falling off while preserving access to the low windowsill.

It's less costly to convert an existing space than to build a bathroom addition. Then again, conversion costs vary depending on the location of plumbing lines and fixtures. The main question in terms of cost is where you'll locate the new toilet. If the new fixture cannot be plumbed into the existing vent stack, the resulting complications can add thousands of dollars to your remodeling cost. Laundry areas are good candidates for conversions because they're already equipped with plumbing. For an attic or basement conversion, it's most economical to stack a new bathroom directly over or under an existing one. Attic conversions may require adding or changing roof trusses or beefing up the roof framing.

Any underused room is an option for becoming a new bath. A spare bedroom is an excellent candidate for conversion. You might also consider combining two small bedrooms into one luxurious master suite. As you plan the new bathroom consider, too, what you will do with the old bathroom space. If it's accessible from other rooms or a hallway, it might function nicely as a family or guest bath. Or, if it's not needed as a bathroom after the new one is complete, you might benefit from a new walk-in closet.

Attention to detail in the planning stages increases the functionality of this bathroom. A pocket door separates the tub and shower space from the vanity area without using precious additional floor space.

PLAN AN ADDITION

Adding a bath to the exterior of your house is generally more expensive than finding room for one inside, but if you don't have space to spare, an addition may be the only choice. In the bath featured here, nostalgic looks complement 21st-century convenience. Despite its newness the homeowners wanted an interior design that had some age to it. Random-width flooring salvaged from a local barn, ironstone pitchers, and tub decking and a shower surround clad in beaded board lend vintage pleasantries.

Planning is critical for an addition, particularly for maximizing space and minimizing costs. Carefully plot all of the elements and fixtures you need in the new bathroom. Then add in some or all of the nice-to-have features. If the anticipated cost exceeds your budget, these are the first items to eliminate. This exercise also helps determine the size of the addition you need. Building to standard sizes will help minimize costs since standard-size vanities and fixtures cost less than custom ones. Uniquely shaped spaces may require custom-built cabinets or shower enclosures to maximize the room's usable space.

Design Tip

Look for ways to add on without disrupting the traffic flow in other rooms. Make the new space match the old as closely as possible. New bath windows, for example, should be the same as or consistent with others in the house. Take design cues from those already in the house.

Cost-Effective Expansion

If an addition is too costly, consider a bumpout as an affordable alternative. This room extender can be cantilevered, and is less expensive because it does not require its own foundation. A cantilevered bumpout typically expands 2 to 4 feet beyond the existing foundation. Any more than a 4-foot overhang generally requires expensive structural supports. Keep this solution in mind if strict building codes prevent you from adding to the foundation.

To achieve ideal results from a bath addition, consider both the interior and exterior. This bath is lined with large windows to capitalize on the mountain views without the fishbowl effect of a room dominated by a vast expanse of glass.

The shower features a curved wall on the outside and a row of massage showerheads inside. The open top permits the shower area to share the light while providing privacy for bathers.

Gain through expansion

To gain more square footage than a small bumpout provides, look for ways to add on without disrupting the traffic flow in other rooms. If an existing bath is at the back of the house and hugs an exterior wall, it might be an ideal candidate for an addition.

Several factors impact an addition. First local building codes determine the restrictions that apply to your home and property. Knowing what you are able to do early in the process allows you to focus your dreams and plans on a viable option. Involving design professionals early in the planning stages may also help you develop solutions that are less disruptive to traffic patterns and that better blend with your home's architecture.

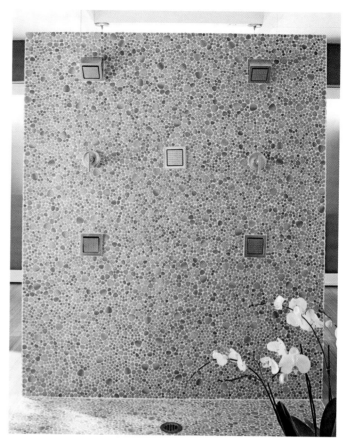

A walk-through shower is universal design-friendly and visually stunning. The shower wall is covered in Italian ceramic tile that resembles stones and is equipped with a shower system that accommodates two bathers.

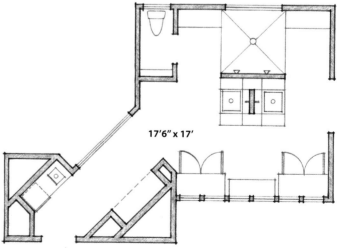

17'6" x 17'

A dressing spot adjacent to the walk-through shower is delineated by beaded paneling that matches the room's custom benches and vanities. A hatbox-style toilet has its own compartment.

Back-to-back sinks ease morning rush hour for a busy couple. The vanities tuck in behind the shower wall.

The luxury of ample floor space allowed this open retreat. Separate vanities frame a tub bay and lend an air of living room elegance. Wavy window glass delivers privacy and light.

FLOOR PLANS

A bath often serves as a space for busy homeowners to recharge, with room for pampering and relaxing. Some designers include amenities such as breakfast bars, beverage stations, and sitting areas. If you dream of such a retreat, the floor plan for your new bath must work extra hard to incorporate these items while leaving enough room for the essentials.

Needs first

Plot the essentials first. If your bathroom must include a separate tub and shower and a private toilet compartment to accommodate everyone who will use it, find places for these items before you include anything optional. It's much more difficult to work backward. Starting with the basics allows you to know how much space remains for the extras. The couple who designed this bath needed a private bathroom they didn't have to share with their two young sons. What they desired was additional closet space, a large shower, and a two-person whirlpool bath; not an easy accomplishment in a small home with only a small hall bath. After numerous drawings they developed a plan for a new master bathroom and hallway in the existing master bedroom area. The hallway leads to a modest master bedroom addition.

Walls and dividers

Depending on your needs and preferences, you may go with a single open space or various divided private areas. In the case of this master bath, interior walls would have taken up too much precious floor space. Instead careful planning delivers modest privacy. The linen cabinetry at the end of the vanity area, for instance, partially conceals the toilet. The partial shower wall necessary for the whirlpool tub installation hides the shower seat from the rest of the room.

Multiple versions of floor plans finally resulted in this bath, part of a master suite that afforded just enough space to incorporate a desired whirlpool tub for two.

Beaded-board wainscoting paired
with garden-inspired wallpaper
sets the fresh cottage tone.

CHAPTER 5

Surfaces

Flooring, Walls and Ceilings, Countertops

A bar-top finish protects this cherry countertop.

You've identified your needs for a renovated or new bathroom, explored style and layout options, considered floor plans, and determined the best strategy to achieve your goals. Perhaps now the real fun begins: selecting the materials, colors, and textures that fill the bath and cast the ambience you desire. In this chapter you'll explore surface choices—floor, wall and ceiling treatments, and countertops—that will promote your personal style and enhance comfort and functionality. Many surface materials come in various forms, some of which are better suited to bathroom wear and tear. For example, ceramic floor tiles are rated by how well they resist water (porosity); for bathroom use you'll want tiles with the highest level of water resistance, a rating of "impervious." Function may trump form, but in this arena you'll discover a range of surface options that are as elegant, fun, or charming as they are durable.

FLOORING

Bath floors, along with kitchen floors, are probably the hardest-working surfaces in your home. They must take plenty of abuse: overflowing sinks and bathtubs, wet feet, heavy foot traffic, garden dirt, and more. To determine what flooring will work best for you, consider three major criteria: what you need in terms of wear and tear, how the floor will fit into your design, and whether your selection will fit your budget.

Bamboo

A popular "green" flooring choice, bamboo is a grass and grows faster than trees; therefore, it's considered more renewable than wood. Like wood, bamboo is very strong. Also like wood, bamboo cannot withstand standing water so splashes must be wiped up quickly. Depending on how bamboo flooring is treated, it may darken with exposure to natural light.

Carpet

Because carpet absorbs water, stains easily, and promotes mildew growth, it is not recommended for bath installations, particularly in areas adjacent to the toilet, tub, or shower. If you like the feel of carpet underfoot, use washable rugs or have a washable or dry-cleanable carpet runner custom-made to cover the vanity's floor area. Nylon and other synthetics are washable; wool is durable but not washable.

Ceramic tile

Clay-base ceramic tiles are the ideal choice for moisture-prone bath areas. Floor tiles are extremely durable, are water, stain, and wear resistant, and easy to care for. They come in an array of colors, patterns, shapes, and sizes. Tile feels cold underfoot but you may install a radiant heat system to warm it. For safety purposes always choose a bath tile that has a slip-resistant finish. Seal all tile grout; otherwise it is difficult to clean. Broken tiles cannot be repaired, but they can be replaced.

Concrete

Able to withstand the rigors of heavy traffic, concrete is becoming a popular surface for much-used areas of the home. Easy to clean and versatile, concrete also can be made to mimic the look of stone at a lower cost than the real thing. It can be dyed virtually any color and before it is fully cured, stamped to create any surface texture or appearance. Because concrete is very porous, it must be sealed for protection against embedded dirt and stains.

Earthy flagstone floor tiles are naturally slip resistant.

Ash floors paired with a mahogany tub enclosure add a warm, rich look to this bath.

Sturdy Floor Support

Before installing a new floor, you must check the condition of the subfloor (the material between the floor covering and the floor joists) and the supporting joists. Decayed subflooring, especially around the toilet and tub, is a common problem in older homes. Spot repairs sometimes suffice, but in some cases, a new subfloor is necessary. Unless you can inspect the underside of the subfloor from the basement, you'll have to pry up a bit of the existing floor covering to inspect the subfloor. Prod the base of fixtures and cabinets with a screwdriver in search of soft spots. Check with a professional if you are unsure how to proceed.

Hardwood

Although not recommended for a family bathroom, wood flooring is definitely a possibility for grown-up spaces. Protected by a durable polyurethane finish, natural wood requires only that you mop standing water quickly. In addition to traditional hardwood species such as oak and maple, exotic options such as cork (whose cushiony surface is prone to dents and gouges) also work well in a master bath. People are most familiar with wood flooring in the form of solid boards. But engineered wood flooring, which consists of two or more layers of wood laminated together like plywood, is a good option. The top layers consist of a hardwood veneer; the bottom layers are typically softer woods. Due to this structure you typically can refinish these engineered woods only once, but many professionals consider them more stable for moisture-filled bath installations. Both engineered and solid woods are wear resistant, and they provide a naturally warm look. Because the floor is softer than ceramic or stone, it is more comfortable to walk on.

Laminate

Laminate is the impersonator of flooring materials. Laminate flooring features a decorative image printed on one or more thin sheets of paper or other fibrous material. The decorative layer, which can mimic wood, ceramic tile, or stone, is impregnated with plastic or resin and bonded to a rigid core for durability. Laminate comes in three shapes: planks, squares, and rectangles. Today's virtually stainproof laminate is easy to clean, never fades, and never needs waxing. Less expensive than its authentic counterparts, laminate feels a bit hollow underfoot. One plus: You can install it over existing flooring. Not all laminates are suitable for installation in moisture-prone rooms, so be sure to check the manufacturer's warranty before purchasing it for your bathroom. Laminate can't be refinished if damaged.

Resilient

All synthetic resin-based floor coverings fall under the resilient flooring category and include vinyl and linoleum flooring. Vinyl is available in tiles and sheet flooring. Sheets up to 15 feet wide eliminate seams in most bathrooms. Linoleum is enjoying a resurgence in popularity and is considered an eco-friendly choice. Resilient flooring is an excellent choice if you have young children because it's flexible, water and stain resistant, and easy to maintain. It's also relatively soft, it helps muffle noise and is easy on the feet and legs. The softness of the flooring, however, makes it likely to dent.

Stone tile

Stone tiles are actually boulders and slabs of natural rock that have been sliced into thin squares or rectangles. Granite tiles require little or no maintenance; they are nonporous, easy to clean, and virtually indestructible. For better traction, choose a honed finish. Not all stone is suitable for use as bath flooring, however. Glossy surfaces require regular polishing and are slippery when wet. Marble tiles require a sealer to prevent staining and pitting. Limestone and slate, also porous, must be sealed to prevent dirt and stain absorption.

Terrazzo floor tiles speckled with seashell-like flecks blend into soft blue cabinetry, setting the stage for a tranquil retreat.

Warmth underfoot

Bathroom floors probably encounter bare feet more than any other room in the house. Some flooring materials are inherently cool, but thanks to radiant heating systems installed between the subfloor and the finish floor your toes can stay toasty on even the coldest mornings. It's possible to install most systems across the entire floor or confine them to a specific area such as in front of a vanity or bathtub. See page 98 for more on radiant heating systems.

Radiant heat warms the limestone and mosaic tiles that otherwise would cause a chill.

Bathroom Flooring Options

MATERIAL	PROS	CONS	COST
Bamboo	• More renewable source than wood • Strong	• May darken when exposed to natural light • Should not be left wet	$5-$7 per sq. ft.
Carpet	• Warm • Moderately priced • Readily available • Variety of colors and styles	• Not good in damp and high-moisture areas • Absorbs water • Promotes mildew growth • Shows dirt in high-traffic areas	$1–$30 per sq. ft.
Ceramic tile	• Durable • Low maintenance • High moisture resistance • Wide choice of colors, designs, and textures	• Cold to the touch • Glazed tiles slippery when wet • Grout lines hard to clean • Unforgiving of dropped objects	$3–$12 per sq. ft.
Concrete	• Extremely durable and long-lasting • Can be stained with color	• Cold to the touch • Unforgiving of dropped objects • Prone to cracking • Requires regular sealing treatments • Quality depends on the installation	$4–$10 per sq. ft. installed. Coloring or acid etching is additional.
Cork	• Soft and warm, natural look • Resists mildew • Does not absorb water	• Finish must be sanded off and reapplied every few years	$4–$9 per sq. ft.
Engineered wood	• Shrinks and expands less than wood • Resists moisture and spills • Installs over many substrates	• Typically can be refinished only once • Shows wear faster than solid wood	$4–$11 per sq. ft.
Laminate	• Resembles natural material • Durable, resists moisture and stains • Easy to clean and maintain • Wide range of colors and designs • Installs over many substrates	• Can't be refinished • Sometimes sounds hollow underfoot	$2–$9 per sq. ft.
Linoleum	• Made of natural raw materials • More durable than vinyl • Color extends through entire material	• Requires sealer • Cannot be left wet	$4-$9 per sq. ft.
Stone	• Natural elegance • Almost indestructible	• Cold to the touch • Must be properly sealed • Susceptible to imperfections • Marble and other glossy stone is slippery • Limestone and granite absorb stains	$3–$30 or more per sq. ft.
Vinyl	• Durable • Water resistant in sheet form • Easy to clean • Comfortable • Less expensive than most flooring choices	• Difficult to repair • Less expensive grades may discolor • In tile form moisture can get into seams between tiles	$1–$5 per sq. ft.
Wood	• Warm, natural look • Can be refinished	• Vulnerable to moisture • Can shrink and expand, creating gaps or warping	$6–$14 per sq. ft.

A black slate tub surround is rugged and water-resistant. Grass cloth framed by cherry 1×4s has a shoji screen effect that lends interesting texture.

WALLS AND CEILINGS

Whether you choose paint, tile, paneling, or wallpaper, your bathroom wallcoverings must stand up to heat, humidity, and frequent cleaning. Mix and match materials to meet your durability requirements. The goal is to come up with a look that is attractive and practical.

Paint

Paint is the least expensive option and the easiest to change when you tire of it. Look for a paint finish that is scrubbable and moisture resistant. Paints specified for bathroom use are more expensive but worth the investment in terms of durability. If you want to cover a porcelain, plastic, or tile surface, look for an epoxy paint made to handle that specific purpose. Most such surfaces must be primed to ensure proper paint adhesion.

Tile

Tile is available in a stunning array of colors, finishes, and patterns. The latest tile trends feature iridescent and metallic finishes, floral patterns, jewellike insets, and organic shapes. Tile can even mimic the look of wood and leather.

Besides making an attractive design statement, ceramic and natural stone tiles boast durability and low-maintenance care. Most are stain resistant and, when installed correctly, fully waterproof. Although tile is more expensive than paint, its longevity makes it worth considering at least for the wettest areas of the bath.

Some wall tiles are glazed, some are not. Unglazed tile must be properly sealed to resist moisture. Wall tiles are not as durable as floor and countertop tiles, so although you may use floor and countertop tiles on the walls, do not use wall tiles to cover countertops or floors.

Trimwork Adds Style

To enhance the style quotient, look beyond ordinary drywall and consider adding architectural details to your bathroom walls. Moldings offer one of the quickest and easiest ways to inject a basic bathroom with an eye-pleasing dose of architectural interest. Crown molding defines the room, while a chair rail dresses the top of wainscoting. A plate rail is handy for displaying a few accessories.

Moldings come in a variety of materials ranging from pine to hardwood to high-density polyurethane. For simple painted molding designs, paint-grade wood is often the best choice. When ornate detail is involved, however, molded polyurethane may be more economical. Whatever selections you make, choose moldings that coordinate with the design of the bathroom and also complement any existing millwork in your house.

Bathtub-friendly beaded-board wainscoting partnered with wallpaper hung high on the wall spell bold style without subjecting the paper to damaging water.

Paneling

Beaded-board wainscoting is a popular choice for the bathroom. For a vintage, cottage, or fresh country look, select white beaded board. For a more rustic or natural look, choose natural stained wood panels.

As a wall-surfacing material, paneling comes in the form of premilled solid wainscoting or tongue-and-groove beaded board, veneered plywood, or melamine-surfaced hardboard. To protect from moisture solid wood and plywood-backed veneers must be sealed with a water-resistant coating such as polyurethane. Hardboard panels coated with melamine (a thin layer of white plastic) are well suited for baths because melamine is water resistant and easy to clean.

Glass and glass block

Glass is often used for shower surrounds and partial walls because it enables light to filter through the entire bath while visually expanding the space. Sandblasted glass provides both privacy and a contemporary finish. Glass block is another well-liked option for bath wall applications because it transmits light while preserving some privacy. Use it to build walls, shower surrounds, and windows.

Vinyl wallcoverings

Vinyl wallcoverings—a more durable choice for the bath than ordinary wallpapers—come in a vast array of colors, patterns, styles, and textures. For use in the bath choose a vinyl covering that is laminated to a fabric backing and avoid coverings that are all or partly paper. Vinyl coverings withstand moisture much better than papers do. Products labeled "scrubbable" are the most durable and will tolerate more abrasion than the "washable" ones. If you have your heart set on a specific standard wallpaper, consider using it in a powder room or in areas of the bath that are not subjected to splashes or condensation.

This bath is rich in mosaic tile. Darker blues and greens cover the shower and tub surrounds. Paler hues line the floor and toilet compartment. The two distinct yet related mosaics harmonize the space without overwhelming it.

Ceiling Adornment

Since the ceiling typically is the largest uninterrupted space in the room, consider how you'll finish that "wall" as well. Any variation from a standard 8-foot-high white ceiling will have a dramatic impact on the overall look of the room. A higher ceiling adds volume to a small space. Painting the ceiling lighter than the walls makes it visually recede. If your bath is especially large and has a high ceiling, you can bring about a more intimate feel by painting the ceiling a shade or two darker than the walls. Another option is to recess the center of the ceiling and install cove lighting around the perimeter. Beaded-board paneling or wood planks yield a warm, rustic look. Covering the ceiling with a faux-finish treatment draws the eye upward. For a historical look, apply tin ceiling panels—most manufacturers offer many patterns and colors. Medallions are another traditional decorative element for ceilings that may be painted or left plain.

Glass wall tiles in a watery color form the lower portion of the wall while sparkling mirrors and their picturesque reflections stretch above the sinks.

COUNTERTOPS

In addition to suiting the style of your bath, countertops must stand up to water, soap, toothpaste, cosmetics, and acetone- and alcohol-base liquids. Materials that are free of seams and sharp corners that catch dirt are the easiest to maintain. Countertops of cultured marble and solid-surface material, for example, offer the option of an integrated sink, which is molded into the countertop, making cleaning a snap. On the other hand, ceramic tile, although durable and beautiful, requires regular maintenance to keep the grout lines clean and mildew-free.

Ceramic tile
As they do for walls and floors, clay-base ceramic tiles make an attractive, durable finish for countertops, especially in moisture-prone areas. The surface tiles are water, stain, and wear resistant. Heat from curling irons won't cause damage.

They are available in an array of colors, patterns, shapes, and sizes. The tiles themselves are easy to care for but, as with tile flooring, unsealed grout is subject to mildew and is difficult to clean.

Concrete
Concrete is a pliable wonder that you can color, score, and texture to come up with whatever impression suits your bath. Inlay decorative tiles and metals or integrate the sink for a custom look. Because concrete is very porous it requires a sealant for protection against embedded dirt and stains.

Laminate
Affordably priced laminate is still the most widely used countertop surfacing material. Available in multiple patterns and colors, laminate offers textures that range from smooth and glossy to mottled and leatherlike. Stone-look finishes are most popular. Laminate countertops clean easily and resist water and stains. However, they are susceptible to scratches, and they wear thin and become dull over time. Hard blows that chip or dent the plastic cannot be repaired.

Quartz (engineered stone) surfacing
Engineered stone—a mixture of natural stone and resins—has the look, feel, and texture of granite and other solid stone materials. One plus: Unlike stone, quartz resists stains. It also does not require sealers and is scratch resistant. Engineered stone has a consistent pattern and color, so the countertop installed in your bath will look exactly like the sample you first saw. You won't get the variations found in natural stone, but manufacturers continue to expand the range of colors, patterns, and textures.

A white marble countertop suits the traditional styling of a washstand-inspired vanity. To retain its creamy hue, marble must be sealed, and stain-producing bath products must be used with caution.

Unique Choices

Though you'll find these countertop materials featured in magazines, you might not have considered them for your own home. If you want to make a style statement in the bath, one of these alternatives can do it:

Metal. Stainless steel is easy to clean and boasts sleek texture but is prone to dents and scratches. It also shows fingerprints easily. Copper, brass, and other metals are possibilities but may scratch and require additional care.

Glass. Glass slabs create a dramatic effect. No need to worry about breakage or safety. Certainly if you drop a heavy object on a glass counter it can break just as tile and other surfaces would, but glass used for countertops is quite thick and fairly durable. The nonporous, seamless material also keeps stains from sinking in and germs from gathering. Frosted glass hides scratches and water spots better than clear glass. Be sure to work with a professional designer and installer experienced in glass.

Used as a flooring surface for thousands of years, terrazzo is also an option for countertops. Terrazzo combines marble or other stone chips with cement and a color pigment to form a durable and attractive surface.

Open space under the countertop offsets the visual weight of gold-tinted concrete and dark wood cabinetry.

Bathroom Countertop Options

MATERIAL	PROS	CONS	COST
Ceramic tile	• Durable • Water and stain resistant • Wide choice of colors, designs, textures, and shapes	• Moisture and dirt get stuck in grout joints • Chips easily • Can stain unless tiles are sealed • Fragile items dropped on the counter will most likely break • Difficult to repair	$18–$140 per linear foot installed
Concrete	• Hard wearing, long-lasting • Easy to clean if properly sealed • Versatile • Can be tinted a wide range of colors	• Prone to staining • Prone to cracking and chipping • Requires regular sealing • Quality depends heavily on the installation	$70–$200 per linear foot installed; staining and etching increase the cost
Laminate	• Durable, inexpensive • Easy to clean and maintain • Wide range of colors and designs	• Can be scratched • Cannot be refinished if damaged	$26–$60 per running foot installed
Quartz (engineered stone) surfacing	• Durable • Wider range of colors than stone • Does not require sealing	• Uniform look unlike look of natural stone • Edges may chip	$50–$85 per square foot installed
Solid-surfacing	• Requires little maintenance • Very durable • Nonporous so moisture and bacteria cannot easily penetrate surface • Scratches, abrasions, and minor burns repaired with fine-grade sandpaper • Available in many colors and styles • Sinks integrated directly into the countertop	• Intense heat and heavy falling objects cause damage • Can be scratched	$100–$250 per linear foot installed
Stone	• Virtually indestructible • Elegant • Some varieties, such as granite, are easy to maintain • Withstands high temperatures	• Expensive • Some varieties, such as marble and limestone, readily absorb stains and dirt • Difficult to repair • Gloss surfaces require regular polishing • Most varieties require sealing periodically	$125–$250 per running foot* * Varies by region depending on how far the stone must be shipped
Wood	• Wear resistant • Long-lasting • Provides a warm look • Surface finish easy to keep clean • Can be refinished	• Vulnerable to moisture • Some woods, such as pine, dent easily • May darken with age • Some finishes wear unevenly and are difficult to repair	$40–$75 per linear foot installed

Solid-surfacing

Cast from an acrylic resin, solid-surfacing countertops require little maintenance and are more durable than laminate. Intense heat and heavy objects that fall on them may cause damage, but scratches, abrasions, and minor burns can be repaired with fine-grade sandpaper. Solid-surfacing countertops are available in more colors and styles than ever before. Edge treatments range from a simple smooth edge that imitates stone to intricate inlaid designs in contrasting colors. Sinks are integrated directly into the countertop, so there are no seams to clean.

Stone tiles and slabs

In general, stone countertops are extremely durable but specific properties vary depending on the variety of stone. Granite, for example, resists stains and stands up well to water. It comes in slab and tile form. Slabs are more expensive but eliminate grout cleanup. Some more porous natural stone varieties, such as limestone and marble, are prone to staining if not kept clean and properly sealed. Marble veining, although attractive, makes the marble weaker than other stone. Cultured marble is made from crushed natural marble that's coated in plastic to produce a hard, water- and stain-resistant surface. Cultured marble is available in sheet form. As with solid-surfacing, cultured marble is a candidate for integrating the sink into the countertop.

Soapstone is an increasingly popular choice for countertops. A virtually impervious surface, soapstone oxidizes from a light gray to dark charcoal. While no finish is necessary, a protective coat of mineral oil is recommended to enhance the natural veining. Most scratches disappear with a dab of mineral oil; even deep scratches are remedied with gentle sanding.

Although you might think twice about using stone countertops in every bathroom in your home, perhaps their maintenance drawbacks and hefty price tag will not dissuade you from enjoying their luxurious colors and textures in your personal bath.

Wood

Wood counters are attractive, versatile, and easy to install, but they are especially vulnerable to water damage. Whatever type of wood you choose must be sealed with a marine-quality polyurethane varnish. Special care must be taken to seal around the edges of plumbing fixtures so standing water can't seep in and cause warping or wood rot.

The limestone countertop and the backsplash pick up the reddish tint of a sumptuous mahogany vanity.

DESIGN GALLERY
Surfaces

In the bathroom, surface materials extend beyond the utilitarian. As a matter of fact, they can serve as art in their own right. Thoughtful selection and application generates visual treats that withstand daily wear.

1. Stately walnut paneling and a furniture-style marble-top vanity prove that traditional design never goes out of style.

2. Stone materials such as these slate wall and floor tiles provide naturally subtle color and earthy texture. A teak vanity supports a shapely sink in this Asian-inspired design.

3. The concrete countertop supports a custom cast concrete sink with a trough-style bowl. Because concrete surfaces are cast on site, the quality depends on the installation.

4. The jewellike quality of iridescent mosaic tiles lends a subtle sense of luxury.

5. Narrow grout lines minimize the work of cleaning and allow color variations in the tile to command attention.

A period-style freestanding tub with a vintage-look faucet is the pitch-perfect choice for a 1920s home.

CHAPTER 6

Fixtures

Sinks and Faucets, Bathtubs,
Showers and Showerheads, Toilets and Bidets

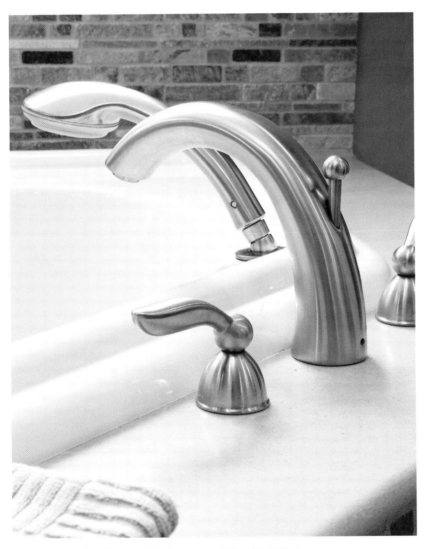

Choosing sinks, faucets, tubs, showers, and toilets involves aesthetic as well as practical decisions. Use your decorating preferences to help you narrow your choices, guiding you toward sink, faucet, and tub styles that contribute to the overall design statement you want to make. You'll also need to consider function, durability, and price. Your best dollar payback will come from equipping your bath with fixtures that have become the standard in comparably priced homes. If you're planning to live in the house for years, however, make fixture choices that are as personal as you please. Today more than ever it pays to consider water usage—new faucets, showerheads, and toilets that use less water will save you money while conserving natural resources.

A clean-line solid-surfacing tub deck serves a whirlpool bath that has a satin nickel faucet and hand shower.

SINKS AND FAUCETS

Bathroom sinks come in more sizes, shapes, and materials than ever. You can purchase round, oval, rectangular, or asymmetrical bowls. Each shape is available in several colors, though white still outsells all of the other colors combined. Some of the more expensive models feature handpainted designs. Or, if you're willing to splurge, you can indulge in a standard sink custom-painted to match your decor.

Before you choose the right one (or two) for your bath, consider how often the sink will be used. Sinks in powder rooms and guest baths get less use, so durability and maintenance are less important considerations.

For frequently used baths, look for low-maintenance fixtures. Larger, deeper sinks reduce splashes and countertop cleanup, for example. To ensure a unified design, consider purchasing a matching sink, toilet, and bathtub.

Sink styles

Sinks fall into three main categories:

Pedestal. These sinks fit on top of a pedestal-shape base and are an ideal solution for a small bath. The disadvantage of a pedestal sink is that it offers little counterspace and no base cabinet storage below. Simple pedestals start at $125.

Wallhung. Like pedestal sinks, wallhung styles have the advantage of squeezing into small spaces. They have the same disadvantages of pedestal sinks with one more: There is no pedestal to hide the plumbing lines. To make up for this, some sinks have brass legs. Wallhung sinks are often the preferred choice in universal design baths because they install at any height and have a clear space underneath that allows for seated knee space and wheelchair access. These sinks start at around $75.

Vanity. Vanity sinks have lots of countertop space around them as well as cabinet storage below. They require the most floor space of any sink style. Vanity sinks are installed in different ways depending on the type of sink you select. See "Sink Installations," right.

Faucets

As you shop for faucets, you'll find everything from traditional two-handle models that rival the designs of a century ago to the newest one-handle designs that look like contemporary sculpture. Faucet prices start at $60 for the most basic models and run as high as $1,000 or more. Solid brass die-cast parts are a sign of quality, but they often come with steep price tags, anywhere from $250 to $1,000 or more. Beware of faucets with plastic shells or handles. Although appealing in price, their longevity is questionable.

Avoid selecting a faucet based on looks alone; durability is the key to your continued satisfaction. Comfort in turning the water on and off is also a factor given how many times you'll use the faucet. You'll also need to make sure the faucet set you select is the proper size and design to fit your sink. Most vanity sinks come with holes drilled in their rims to accommodate standard faucets and plumbing.

A vessel sink rests on top of the counter like a bowl. A gooseneck faucet maximizes space available for hand washing.

Sleek stainless-steel sinks are available in several finishes, from a mirrorlike shine to a satiny luster. They pair perfectly with wallmount faucets.

Sink Installations

SINK TYPE	INSTALLATION	DETAILS	COST
Vessel	• Most rest in a custom-cut hole in the vanity top	• Makes a dramatic design statement • Sits on top of the vanity counter	$300–$700 for most models
Integral	• One piece with the vanity counter	• Easy to clean because there is no joint between the bowl and countertop • If damaged beyond repair the entire unit must be replaced	$200–$500
Self-rimming or surface-mount	• Top edge rests on top of the counter after the sink is dropped into a hole large enough to accommodate the sink bowl • Rim forms a tight seal with the countertop to prevent leaks	• Easiest to install • The hole need not be a perfect cut because it is hidden below the rim once the sink is in place	Start at $50
Undermount	• Attached to the bottom of the countertop • Requires an exact cut for installation	• Clean look • Difficult to clean underneath the lip where the sink and counter seal • Requires a near-perfect cut for installation	Start at $60
Rimmed	• Sits slightly above the countertop • A tight-fitting metal rim joins the sink and countertop	• The rim is made of different finishes to match faucet type	Start at $70

Three basic faucet styles are designed to fit predrilled holes:

Single-handle faucets. These faucets have one spout and one handle that controls the flow of both hot and cold water.

Center-set faucets. With a spout and handle(s) in one unit, these faucets may have either single-handle or double-handle controls. Most are designed for a three-hole basin, with the outside holes spaced 4 inches from center to center. However some have a single-post design that requires only one hole.

Spread-fit faucets. These faucets have separate spout and handles. The connection between them is concealed below the sink deck. They fit holes spaced 4 to 10 inches apart. You have even more options when they are mounted on a countertop next to the sink. For example, you can place the spout on a rear corner and the handles off to one side. These faucets are handy for tight installations where there is not enough room for a full faucet at the back of the sink basin. They are also ideal for whirlpool tubs because the handles can be positioned where they are easily accessible from outside the tub for filling.

Wallmount faucets. A fourth faucet type is attached to the wall instead of the sink or the counter. These faucets are designed for unusually shaped sinks, such as vintage farm sinks, antique bowls, or other vessels that have been modified for use in the bath.

Sinks

SINK MATERIAL	PROS	CONS
Porcelain-enameled cast iron	• Extremely durable • Easy to care for	• Somewhat heavy • Requires a sturdy support system
Vitreous china	• Lustrous surface • Not as heavy as porcelain cast-iron sinks • Most resistant to discoloration and corrosion	• Can be chipped or cracked when struck by a heavy object
Solid-surfacing	• May be integrated directly into the countertop • Fine-grade sandpaper removes shallow nicks and scratches	• Offers varying degrees of durability based on the material from which it is made • Sinks made from the same acrylic resin as quality solid-surfacing countertops are more durable and require little maintenance • Polyester and cultured marble sinks share similar properties but scratch and dull more readily
Stainless steel	• Durable • Unaffected by household chemicals	• Tends to show hard-water and soap spots
Glass	• Smooth finish is easy to clean • Frosted glass shows water spotting less than its clear counterpart	• Requires extra care to prevent scratching or breaking • Shows water spotting

A shallow rectangular sink installed on top of the counter offers a trendy variation on the vessel sink. The gooseneck faucet spans the space between mirror and sink for a sculptural effect.

These console sinks, a freestanding alternative to pedestal sinks, each have four legs and modest storage in the form of a shelf below the sink. Console sinks with two legs are also available but typically do not offer undersink storage.

Faucet Finishes

FINISH OPTION	PROS	CONS
Chrome (polished, brushed, or matte)	• Extremely hard • Easily cleaned • Doesn't oxidize • Matte chrome has a softer appearance and is as durable as polished chrome	• Inexpensive chrome sprayed over plastic parts tends to peel
Brass (polished, satin finish, or antique finish)	• Titanium finishes resist scratching, fading, and corrosion	• Standard brass finishes are prone to scratching, tarnishing, and corrosion
Baked-on enamel or epoxy coatings	• Wide choice of colors • Easy to clean	• May chip or fade • Some chemicals may damage color
Gold plate (polished, brushed, or matte)	• Visual appeal • Quality gold won't tarnish • Matte finishes hide scratches	• Expensive • Quality varies • Manufacturer must seal finish to prevent damage
Other metals (polished, brushed, or matte)	• Metals such as nickel offer visual appeal and durability	• Can be expensive • Quality varies

Design Tip

When selecting a sink for your bath, consider frequency of use. An easy-to-clean sink is more crucial in an often-used bath than in a showy powder room. How your sink is attached to the countertop affects ease of cleaning too. Both integral and undermount sinks make it easy to wipe messes from the counter into the sink. Self-rimming sinks, on the other hand, have a perimeter lip sealed with a base of caulk that easily collects dirt.

A cantilevered sink with a spread-fit faucet takes up minimal vanity space—a good idea for a small bath.

Bracketed by high windows, this built-in tub enjoys a sunny yet private spot. A marble deck, paneled surround, and vintage-look wainscoting blend elements from farmhouse and English country styles.

BATHTUBS

If you're replacing a bathtub because you want a larger model or want to replace your current one with a deep soaking tub or whirlpool, keep several points in mind. Is the new model large enough for you to sit in comfortably? Will it fit the space available in your bathroom? Will it fit through your existing doorways? Bear in mind that most bathroom floors can handle 40 pounds of weight per square foot. A large-capacity tub may require extra bracing so that the floor can support it once it is filled with water.

If you're installing a whirlpool, you'll also need access to the pump (typically installed near one end of the tub) in case repairs are necessary. For the best whirlpool bath experience, choose a pump that is quiet and offers a wide range of massage options.

Frosted-glass panels provide privacy for a tub without blocking light. This tub base is fir, and the decking is a soapstone-look composite made from recycled paper and resins that stands up to splashes.

...s

...l and standard bathtubs come in four basic

...sed tubs. With one finished side, called an apron, a recessed tub fits between two end walls and against a back wall. A drain at either end fits your plumbing needs. People with limited mobility may find it difficult to get in and out of these tubs.

Corner tubs. Spacesaving corner tubs fit diagonally between two corners and, like standard apron tubs, have only one finished side. Other corner options have a finished side and one round, finished end.

Freestanding tubs. These tubs are finished on all four sides and can be placed almost anywhere in the room. Claw-foot varieties look appropriate in traditional and vintage baths. You can also find newer styles—such as pedestal designs—that cater to contemporary design.

Platform tubs. These unfinished tubs drop into a platform. The platform's design determines whether the tub belongs in a corner, against a long wall, or in the center of the room.

Bathtubs cost about $150 for a basic 5-foot model and can cost more than $5,000 for a high-end whirlpool.

A tub made of scagliola is the centerpiece of this bath. The smooth stone elevates the tub from a plumbing fixture to an architectural feature.

Design Tip

Can't find a standard tub that suits your needs? Forgo the ordinary for a custom-made stone or tile enclosure with conveniences designed specifically for you. Want to take it a step further? Custom-contoured tubs are built to fit your body shape.

A wall between the tub and shower provides installation space for this corner-style whirlpool tub.

Tub Materials

MATERIAL CHOICE	DETAILS	PROS	CONS
Enameled cast iron	• Iron is molded into a bathtub shape • Finished with enamel	• Thicker than other materials • Retains the heat of the water very well • Durable and solid • Variety of colors	• Heavy • You may need to reinforce the flooring before the tub is installed
Enameled steel	• Enamel is sprayed onto molded steel and fired at a high temperature	• Less expensive than cast iron • Not as heavy as cast iron	• Chips more readily • Fewer colors • Can be noisy to fill with water
Fiberglass	• Fiberglass backing material is finished with a layer of polyester • Wood or metal reinforcement is added to make the tub feel solid	• Inexpensive • Wide choice of styles and shapes • Lightweight	• Polyester finish is not as durable as acrylic • Does not retain heat well
Acrylic	• Sheets of acrylic are heated and formed into a mold, then reinforced with fiberglass and a wood or metal backing	• Wide choice of styles and shapes • Holds heat better than fiberglass if properly insulated	• More expensive than fiberglass • Finish can scratch
Cast polymer	• Solid-color polymer-base materials form tubs that look like natural stone, such as granite or marble	• Thicker than acrylic • Holds heat well	• Not as durable as acrylic or enameled cast-iron tubs

This tub is a modern take on the traditional claw-foot design.
The wallmount faucet furthers its contemporary appeal.

Design Tip

The National Kitchen and Bath Association recommends that the capacity of a hot water heater equal at least two-thirds that of the tub: A 60-gallon hot water tank will serve a 90-gallon tub adequately, for instance, but the rest of the water in the house will be cold.

If your hot water heater is too small, you can either install a bigger heater or install two linked heaters side by side. You can also buy a whirlpool tub with an in-line heater. Instead of heating water before use, like a hot water tank does, an in-line heater maintains the temperature of the water for the duration of your bath. If you plan to soak for long periods, an in-line heater is a good idea regardless of the capacity of your hot water heater.

Your tub's manual will tell you how many gallons of water it will take to fill it.

Luxurious: This whirlpool tub includes deep- and standard-soaking areas as well as a cool-off area.

...e and budget allow for a separate shower, luxury ...lt. Separate fixtures mean two people can bathe at the same time. Shower stalls are also easier to get in and out of and easier to clean than combination tub-shower units. If space and budget are limited, you can make a combination unit safer by selecting a nonslip tub floor and grab bars.

Shower stalls

There are three basic types of shower stalls:

Prefabricated stalls. Available in a variety of shapes and colors, these stalls come in one-, two-, and three-piece versions. They are usually made of fiberglass with a finish surface of acrylic or other plastic, but stalls made of tempered glass combined with fiberglass are also available. Sizes range from 32 inches square (not large enough to meet some local building codes) to 36×48 inches. One-piece versions typically work only for new construction and additions because they are difficult to get through door openings. (Two- and three-piece models readily fit within most door openings.) Doors (or curtains) typically are sold separately. Some units come with their own pan, or flooring piece, while others require a separate pan.

Prefabricated stalls are available in three shapes that are designed to fit against a wall or into a corner: square, rectangular, and neo-angle. Neo-angle models have two finished sides and a diagonal front. Most prefabricated units are made of fiberglass finished with either an acrylic or polyester gel coat. Their walls must attach to standard wall framing for support. Prefabricated stalls range from about $250 for acrylic to $1,000 or more for glass.

Prefabricated shower pans. You'll find molded flooring pieces in a range of materials from plastic to stone. They work with prefabricated shower stalls or custom-made acrylic plastic, solid-surfacing walls, or tiled shower walls. Prices start at about $150.

Custom-made stalls. There's no limit here so build it according to your needs and desires. Choose your favorite waterproof material to cover walls. Consider tile, marble, solid-surfacing, tempered glass, or glass blocks. Prices vary greatly depending on materials used as well as the size and complexity of the design.

A custom shower fits into the corner of this bath. Niches in the wall provide a place to store toiletries.

Designed for two people, this shower features two entrances, two sets of multihead sprays, and a bench in each corner.

A triangular shower turns an awkward corner into a design asset. The frameless door is the next best thing to invisibility.

Showerheads

A growing trend in showers points to a combination of showerheads as opposed to a single wallmount unit. Showerheads are rated according to flow rate, or the number of gallons of water they spray per minute (gpm). Water-consuming showerheads deliver as many as 8 gpm. Low-flow models use only 2.5 gpm while matching the effectiveness of their water-consuming counterparts. Your water pressure plays a part as well. Both types of showerheads adjust to produce a spray that varies from fine to coarse and a water action that ranges from gentle pulsation to vigorous massage.

The following types of spray heads are available:

Standard wallmount showerhead. The most economical option, these heads can be adjusted slightly by moving the shower neck. Models that offer varying spray types fit the needs of most users.

Top-mount showerhead. These showerheads work well in areas where the ceiling is too low to accommodate a wallmount head. Because the spray comes from overhead, showering without getting your hair wet is a challenge.

Handheld showerhead. The 3- to 6-foot-long gooseneck hose attached to these showerheads enables you to hold the showerhead and direct the spray of water, a handy advantage when it comes to washing your hair, rinsing off, or scrubbing the shower enclosure.

Sliding bar showerhead. These showerheads slide up and down on a bar mounted on the wall. Because the height of the spray is easy to adjust, it's a good option when the heights of the people using the shower vary significantly.

Body spray and body mist shower sprays. Heads or sprays installed in vertical rows on opposite or adjacent walls create a crisscross water massage between the knee and shoulder levels. Users can quickly wash without getting their hair wet.

Body spa shower panels. These panels are installed against one or more walls of the shower stall and are equipped with water jets arranged vertically from knee to neck level. Similar to a whirlpool tub, the water jets pump out and recirculate quantities of water for a powerful massage.

Most showerhead-faucet handle combinations cost $75 for a standard model to $2,500 and more for shower towers with multiple sprayers.

Design Tip

Include a bench in your shower where you can sit and relax or enjoy the benefits of a steam shower. If you're building a custom-made shower, a built-in bench will fit easily in your plans. If not, a freestanding bench works too—just make certain it's sturdy and won't slip on the wet floor. Teak is a good type of wood to use for a bath bench because it's naturally water resistant.

A glass enclosure opens this shower to natural light. Multiple body sprays and a limestone bench help create a haven for relaxation.

Steam Showers

Take a trip to the spa without leaving your home. It's easy to do when you have a shower stall that doubles as a steam bath. To make your shower steam-ready:

Equip your shower stall with a top and a door that seals tightly.

Install a vapor barrier on the ceiling and wall framing to prevent moisture, which causes wood rot, from reaching the studs and joists.

Include a steam generator outside the shower. A steam generator heats water from your water system using an electric 220-volt heating element. The size of the generator you'll need depends on the size of your room and the material covering the shower walls. The steam generator supplier will help you determine the best size.

Quartz pebbles outlined with amber glass strips and quartz pebble flooring accent the split-faced quartz interlocking tiles that form the walls of this shower.

Luxury showers combine more than one type of showerhead. This one features an overhead rain shower, a row of massage showerheads, and a sliding bar showerhead.

Design Tip

When selecting toilets, consider cleanup. Unbroken lines make one-piece toilets easier to clean than two-piece models. Wide bowls require less scrubbing than narrow ones because the wider design does a better job of clearing waste. Toilets with straight sides that hide the bolts that secure them to the floor are also easier to wipe clean than those with more curves.

A sleek wallmount toilet leaves only the bowl and panellike flush mechanism visible in the room—a boon for saving space in a small bath.

Low-Flow Toilet Options

TYPE	DETAILS	PROS	CONS	COST
Gravity-flush	• The weight of the water flowing down from the tank clears the bowl • Most manufacturers recommend about 25 pounds per square inch of water pressure for best results	• Least expensive low-flow option • Relatively easy to clean • Newer models use as little as 0.8 to 1.4 gallons per flush	• Does not discharge waste as effectively as other options • Neighborhood and household activities, such as turning on lawn sprinklers, affect the available water pressure	Starts near $150
Pressure-assisted	• Pressurized air created from a vessel hidden in the toilet tank forces water into the bowl and down the drain	• Most effective low-flow option	• Noisier than gravity-flush • More expensive to repair	One-piece units start around $225
Pump-assisted	• An electric pump propels water into the bowl and down the drain	• Quieter than pressure-assisted toilets and works nearly as well	• Most expensive	Starts around $600

TOILETS AND BIDETS

A toilet may be utilitarian but that doesn't mean it can't be stylish. Design choices range from classic two-piece models to sleek low-profile wallmount styles. Choose a toilet that fits your comfort level and the look you seek to broadcast. Whether you are purchasing all new fixtures or just one, make sure the unit you select matches or complements the color and style of the other fixtures in your bath.

Models with elongated bowls are more comfortable than standard round toilets, but they may cost slightly more. Most toilet seat heights range from the standard 14 inches to 17 inches. A toilet seat height of 19 inches is often recommended in universal design guidelines because it's more comfortable for tall people or people with disabilities.

The lowdown on low-flow

By law toilets manufactured after January 1, 1994, may use no more than 1.6 gallons of water per flush. Early low-flow models did not work very well and often required more than one flush to do the job. Today's low-flow toilets, however, are just as reliable as higher-powered models.

If you want to keep your current toilet but would like to reduce its water consumption, you can displace some of the water in the tank by placing a water-filled plastic bottle in the tank. Or install a dual flusher that allows a half-flush for liquid-only flushes.

The bidet

Bidets are used more widely in Europe than in the United States, but they are gaining in popularity here. The fixture resembles a toilet but works more like a sink. Water ascends from the center of the bowl to rinse off the posterior of the person sitting on the bowl.

Unlike a toilet a bidet requires hot and cold water as well as a drain. For convenience locate the bidet close to the toilet. If the two fixtures are installed side by side, leave at least 15 inches between them. Allow at least 3 square feet of floor space for the bidet.

Combination toilet and bidet units are available for $3,000 to $5,000. If you don't have the space or the budget for a separate bidet, a bidet seat may be the answer. These models replace most toilet seats and offer a washing and bidet nozzle. Prices are approximately $700.

Pairing a bidet with a toilet allows access to both conveniences within close proximity.

DESIGN GALLERY
Luxury Fixtures

Bathroom fixtures have moved beyond the basics. Today's striking new options function as well as, if not better than, their standard counterparts. Personal comfort and high style are the orders of the day.

1. Marble seats encourage bathers to linger in a shower that also functions as a steam room.

2. A steam shower dominated by white marble and frosted glass provides spalike elegance.

3. A ceiling-mounted bath filler makes a dramatic statement.

4. Tower shower systems have it all—including hand showers and multiple body sprays.

5. A circular stainless-steel soaking tub produces a cool minimalist effect.

6. Custom-contoured tubs echo the curves of an individual's body for maximum comfort.

A traditional white-painted vanity with bowl sinks and marble countertops ensures that both users have ample storage space.

CHAPTER 7

Cabinetry & Storage

Storage Planning, Organization Strategies,
Cabinetry, Shelves, Medicine Cabinets,
Accessories, Media Options

A mix of open and closed storage maximizes the area under a sink. Open shelves are ideal
for stowing towels because they're easy to access even with wet hands.

The right amenities for organizing and storing bath essentials are crucial to devising a restful haven and an efficient place to start the day. As you peruse this chapter, consider how the broad range of storage options will enhance the functionality of the room and contribute to your desired look for the space. Think big and little: from traditional cabinetry, freestanding and wallmount shelves, and medicine cabinets to towel bars, soap dishes, and toilet paper dispensers. Cabinetry and storage are the nuts and bolts of the operation.

STORAGE PLANNING

The key to keeping a bath tidy is to make putting something away as easy as leaving it on the counter. Plan storage that makes it simple to stay organized and, once your bathroom is complete, you'll save time, space, and money. A smart plan for bath storage should also help simplify your life.

Designate space

To have enough room for everything you need, first determine what you have to store. Plan a specific place for each thing. Though a stack of towels might fit behind small containers of lotion, you'll probably knock over the

Even stock cabinetry typically provides the option of customizing door and drawer inserts and pullouts. These pullout shelves maximize storage.

containers each time you reach for a towel. You'll have an easier time accessing items and getting into the habit of putting things away if you plan a spot for each item.

Proximity

Whenever possible store items right where they are used. For example, the best place for a hair dryer is in an appliance garage where you can keep it plugged in and ready to use. Store your toothbrush, toothpaste, and mouthwash close enough to the sink so that you can grab them without even looking or stepping away.

This lower cabinet built into a cove wall has a pullout laundry hamper.

A mix of storage options provides lots of style and convenient places to house everything from towels to toiletries. Gathered fabric on the bottom of the vanity disguises plumbing.

ORGANIZATION STRATEGIES

Various storage options—vanities, cabinetry, shelves, baskets, hampers, bins, towel racks, medicine cabinets—are available to corral your bath items. To make smart decisions about the storage that will best meet your needs, consider these basic strategies for keeping the room organized.

Keep it simple
When you have to open a door, stoop down, and reach to the back of a base cabinet to reach something you use every day, chances are you won't take the time to put it away when you're finished. Plan to store frequently used items in convenient locations.

Prioritize placement
Assign storage space to items based on frequency of use. Store things used for special occasions at the back of the cabinet or in a linen closet. Stow cleaning supplies below the sink (use childproof mechanisms if necessary).

Make it comfortable
It's easier on your back to reach into a drawer and grab a towel than it is to bend down and pull one out of a base cabinet. Look for vanities with drawers deep enough to hold towels and washcloths. Or consider installing pullout shelves (like those intended for kitchens) in a deep base cabinet. For safety purposes plan to store heavier items in lower spots and lighter items in the high ones.

A mix of open and closed storage allows easy access to frequently used items such as towels and bath lotions. The tall, narrow cupboard takes advantage of otherwise wasted space between the tub and wall.

Kitchen Principles for the Bath

Borrow some tips from kitchen design to fashion a cabinetry and storage plan that works for your bath. Good kitchen design focuses on activity zones: most commonly food prep, cooking, and cleanup. Each zone has its own function and its own accoutrements with accompanying storage needs. Likewise a bathroom typically has at least two zones: bathing and grooming.

Open storage works well in the bathing zone, keeping necessities at hand near the tub and shower. It also prevents having to open drawers or doors with wet hands. Towels can be draped over racks, stacked on a shelf, or rolled and stowed in a large basket. Smaller bathing supplies, shampoos, and soaps feel at home in a niche carved into the tub or shower surround.

In the grooming zone a combination of open and closed storage tends to function best and keeps the bathroom from overflowing with clutter. If the new bath will feature expansive countertops, select attractive trays, baskets, and bins that allow you to easily access daily-use items yet keep them organized. Closed storage—drawers, cabinets, and pullouts—allows you to tuck away toiletries that you don't want on display when they're not in use. For more information about cabinetry, see pages 160–163.

Put wasted space to work

As you plan your bathroom project, look for opportunities to squeeze storage into any available space. A niche between wall studs can house perfume bottles, lotions, and powders, for example. Narrow shelves secured to the inside of base cabinet doors are good for lightweight toiletries.

Add seating

Install a built-in bench where you can sit to pull on socks and shoes. Add drawers below to hold socks and undergarments so you can quickly dress after a bath or shower. If space is too tight for a built-in unit, look for a compact freestanding seat with or without a storage component.

Create a spot for dirty clothes

Unless you have space for a separate dressing area, the bath is likely where dirty clothes pile up. If your bath is next to the laundry room, install a small top-swing door between the two rooms so you can toss clothes directly into a hamper on the laundry room side. If the laundry is below the bath, add a clothes chute so you don't have to carry dirty laundry down the stairs. If neither of these is an option, upgrade a cabinet to include a slide-out hamper, ideally one that is large enough to store the amount of dirty clothes that usually gathers before you wash a load. Install hooks to hold clothes while you shower or bathe.

Commit to a clutter-free bath

Even the best storage plan is only as good as the person who uses it. Don't fill every spot. If storage is limited, follow this rule: one new thing in, one old thing out.

Rotating medicine cabinets deliver style and storage. Mirrors on one side aid grooming, while shelves on the other side store toiletries. Towel bars under the sinks use otherwise wasted space and coordinate with the drawer pulls.

CABINETRY

To begin selecting cabinetry, look at the floor plans you sketched early in the planning process. A successful bath design will optimize storage space but maintain a comfortable floor plan. You don't want cabinetry to encroach on floor space in front of the tub, toilet, and sink. (See pages 75–77 for bathroom space guidelines.) Next, look at the list of specific items you need to store in the bath—from toiletries and grooming aids to towels, cleaning supplies, and toilet paper—to determine how many cabinets you need.

Vanity first

Start with the vanity. This area often serves as a focal point for a bathroom and helps define the entire design. The modest single-sink vanity cabinet has given way to a host of options from double-sink vanities to custom storage hutches to wallmounted cabinets that go far beyond the typical medicine cabinet. The vanity is a natural place to merge form and function, particularly in a master or family bath.

When planning the vanity allow enough room in the front for the doors and drawers to open and close without interference. Make sure you allot enough wall space for a mirror and light fixtures. If either side of the vanity is exposed and a corner juts into the room, consider curved edges to prevent painful bumps from occurring. Once you have met basic space requirements, choose a cabinetry style that suits your design sensibilities. Bath cabinets are available in an ever-increasing array of styles, materials, and colors. The bathroom is one of the most private rooms in the house, so it's a good spot to maximize a look you like.

Hardware

Often overlooked in bath planning, stylish hardware accessorizes a bath and contributes significantly to the finished ensemble. Think of hardware as an ideal way to customize a room. Playful pieces are ideal for children's baths, and more sophisticated pulls suit master or guest baths. When tastes change the hardware is also easy to change.

To find exactly the right cabinetry handles and pulls, search catalogs, home improvement stores, and the Internet. You'll find as many choices as prices. Consider the function and the look of the hardware. While some elaborate designs are attractive, unusual shapes may prove difficult to grasp, and ornate designs may be an ideal spot for grime to accumulate. When you find a style you like, test how comfortable it is in your hand when you open and close a drawer.

Specialty hardware such as this decorative cast bronze handle is generally expensive so mix it with more standard styles.

In a high-drama bath an antique French bookcase stylishly stands in where a bank of built-in cabinetry might have appeared in a more typical design. For safety anchor tall freestanding pieces to the wall.

Clutter meets its match in this master bath and dressing room. Mahogany cabinetry with custom detailing conceals volumes of storage. A built-in armoire adjacent to the vanity stores clothes.

Bath versus kitchen cabinets

No rule bans the use of kitchen cabinets in the bath. The only difference is that vanity cabinets are typically 29 to 30 inches high and kitchen base cabinets are typically 36 inches high. Similarly vanity cabinets' front-to-back depth is 18 to 21 inches and the front-to-back depth of kitchen cabinets typically runs 24 inches. Many people find the 36-inch height more comfortable for standing. If the people who share the bathroom are of significantly different heights, you may want to use a standard bath cabinet for one vanity and a standard kitchen cabinet for another.

Stock versus custom

As with kitchen cabinets, you can purchase bath cabinets in modular (stock) units or with semicustom options, or you can have them custom-designed and built. Most stock vanity widths start at 18 inches and continue in 6-inch increments to 72 inches. Matching filler pieces can be used to adapt a standard vanity to fit almost any space, so even with stock cabinets you can maximize the particular dimensions of your bath. Semicustom cabinets are similar to stock cabinets in that they come in standard styles and finishes, but they offer more sizes, usually within 3-inch increments. Cabinets that are designed and built for a specific bath are custom-made. How the cabinets are made and what the cabinets are made from directly affects the price. Stock cabinets typically are the least expensive and custom the most expensive, with price ranges for each depending on the material, construction, finish, and accessories.

Design Tip

To minimize cleaning chores select easy-clean cabinetry. Cabinets that have flat doors with a baked-on finish are easiest to clean. Choose cabinet pulls and handles that keep you from getting the cabinet surface dirty. D-shape pulls work nicely and let you open the door or drawer with one finger. Drawers that contain potentially messy items, such as toothpaste, benefit from removable liners that clean up in the dishwasher or laundry.

Custom-built cabinetry with translucent resin door panels shows off neatly stacked towels and opaque resin panels conceal the less tidy items.

To preserve the beauty of a jewellike window, a simple oval mirror serves the sink. Nearby adjustable shelves offer storage that a countertop or medicine cabinet typically supply.

SHELVES

Many bathroom items are suitable for storage and display on a shelf. Rolled towels, soaps, and pretty bottles of lotions and perfumes are decorative and functional. Keeping such items on a shelf makes it easier to access them when your hands are wet. Consider the range of storage options:

On the wall

Wallmount shelves are ideal because they provide storage without taking up floor space. For easiest access to items, mount shelves between chin and knee level. Display decorative items that you won't often use on a narrow plate rack near the ceiling. This way they won't get bumped during the morning rush.

Standing room only

Freestanding shelves are another option. Stainless-steel and chrome-plated shelving units impart a sleek, urban air and are easily moved when storage needs or design tastes change. Some of these units come in a variety of styles and with accessories including adjustable hooks to keep wet washcloths off the vanity. You can also put to good use a bookcase. Coat the wood with a sealer to protect against humidity.

Recessed nooks

Adjustable shelves enable you to customize wall niches or nooks to accommodate items of varying heights. To keep shampoo, conditioner, and soap bottles from overtaking the shower or bathtub, plan to include at least one shelf niche in a custom shower surround or tub alcove. Have a coordinating niche in the wall near the vanity to display decorative soaps and pretty containers.

> **Design Tip**
>
> Though shelves offer ample space, without organization items on the shelves can become a jumbled heap. Once you have a list of what you will store on the shelves, use organizers to group similar things. Clear canisters are ideal for small products such as cotton balls and diminutive soaps. Use flat trays or baskets to house grooming supplies such as combs, brushes, and shavers. Small round bins are good candidates for makeup brushes or toothpaste and toothbrushes.

Rustic plank shelves hold a bounty of bathroom essentials. Smaller containers, such as these baskets and glass jars, in conjunction with open shelves make it a cinch to keep items organized.

MEDICINE CABINETS

Aside from the sink, toilet, and shower or tub, a medicine cabinet is probably the most common fixture in a bathroom. Medicine cabinets are ideal for storing small items such as makeup, toothpaste, and other compact toiletries. Most feature a mirror on the front for grooming purposes, though some have beaded-board or flat panel wood fronts. As with most other products for the home, choices for medicine cabinets are expanding so determine your needs and style preferences before making a selection.

Installation type

In their most basic form, medicine cabinets are made two ways: recessed or wallmount. A recessed cabinet fits into the wall between studs and requires little space. A wallmount unit attaches to the surface of the wall and therefore projects farther into the room than a recessed one. Opt for a wallmount medicine cabinet if the wall above the sink contains plumbing, wiring, or other obstructions that would be difficult and costly to move.

Lighting

Though medicine cabinets with integrated lighting above the cabinet are becoming a thing of the past, they're a good solution in rooms where lighting is at a minimum. You'll find models with two or more round bulbs across the top or slim profile fluorescent bulbs down each side. To better see inside the cabinet, some models have an interior mirror on the back and inside door of the cabinet to reflect light.

Design Tip

It's best not to store medicine in the bathroom's medicine cabinet. Excessive heat and humidity can damage medications. It's better to store your prescriptions in a secured, dark, low-humidity area outside the bathroom.

Before purchasing a recessed medicine cabinet, such as this one, make sure the wall above the sink is obstruction free.

ACCESSORIES

Beyond cabinetry, shelving, and medicine cabinets, a plethora of accessories promises to enhance the organizational effectiveness and style of your bath. Small pieces, such as soap dishes, tissue and toilet paper dispensers, tumblers, and swab holders, house bath necessities while infusing the space with personality. When choosing a towel bar, go for a sturdy model that will hold as many towels as you need. Or install multiple rings to hold multiple towels. Don't forget to include a robe hook; the terry wrap that hangs on it is typically the second thing you reach for after bathing. Select accessories that further your unique bath decor.

Store more

Think large as well as small when it comes to accessories. For instance, freestanding furniture pieces, such as a chest of drawers, add convenience to your dressing routine. Maximize each piece's storage capacity by customizing the drawers to fit the specific items you plan to store.

Be creative

Use a jewelry box to store cosmetics and hair accessories. A tiered plant stand makes a good holder for towels, soaps, and other necessities. An open storage and display hutch fits nicely between two sinks. Plan open storage niches for the more attractive items you need to store.

Design Tip

A few simple elements take a bath from ordinary to indulgent. First select soothing colors and surfaces that are pleasing to the touch. Splurge on plush Egyptian cotton towels and scatter scented candles throughout the room. If you have the space, potted plants or bouquets of flowers freshen the space. Keep pampering body scrubs, loofahs, and bath oils within reach of the tub and have plush slippers and a fluffy robe ready when you emerge from the bath or shower.

Freestanding furniture has become a trend in today's bathrooms. This footstool keeps towels within easy reach of the bath.

MEDIA OPTIONS

As baths evolve under the influence of technology, they are becoming more than just a place to shower and shave. Media options are quickly finding a place in the bathroom. Though just about any tub suffices for relaxing with a book or magazine, media-enhanced baths often include televisions and in-wall speakers connected to sound systems.

Television

The sleek flat-panel TV could not be much easier to install—just hang it on the wall. A big-screen plasma unit is too large for most bathrooms; try a 15-inch LCD flat-panel TV. Low-voltage, water-resistant televisions—not widely available—come complete with water-resistant remotes and are designed for installation near a bathtub. Or you can install a standard television high on the wall where

A small makeup counter between the vanities offers enough surface space for a small electronic display screen. Outlets in the bathroom must be GFCI, a particularly critical safety feature if media are positioned near potentially wet surfaces.

water won't splash the screen. Choose a place that enables you to easily catch a glimpse from anywhere in the room. Use mirror reflections to your advantage to maximize the viewing area and make sure the TV is plugged into a ground fault circuit interrupter (GFCI) outlet. To keep the TV in good working order, you'll also need to keep humidity levels in check with proper ventilation. See page 181 for more about ventilation.

Audio

To maximize sound quality install two speakers in opposite corners of the room. Furthermore, keep the speakers at least 2 feet from the corners. If the room is large, consider additional speakers. For the most inconspicuous look, mount in-wall speakers in the wall or in the ceiling. Another option, wallmount speakers, attach to the face of the wall. They have the advantage of adjustable speaker heads that direct sound where you want it to go; the disadvantage is that they project from the wall and are more visually apparent.

Wiring for Media

The best time to figure out what wiring scheme is needed for media in your bath is during the planning stages. If you wait until after the bath is complete, you'll have the mess and expense of running cable through a finished room.

If you're working with professionals, be sure to tell them your plans for media. In addition to making essential safe electrical plans in advance, a TV or in-wall speakers might affect other decisions such as where to place an exhaust fan and what type of fan is installed.

You'll usually need a dedicated outlet for the TV, especially since it's best to position the screen high on the wall where you probably wouldn't find an outlet. Talk with a designer about the best location for the screen and then discuss placement with the electrician so the best route for wiring the TV outlet can be planned. If a stereo system with in-wall speakers is part of your plan, choose thicker speaker wire. Thin wire may compromise sound quality.

Mounting the television high in the corner of this bathroom protects it from splashes. It also allows a clear view of the screen from most points in the room.

DESIGN GALLERY
Details & Specialty Storage

Look beyond standard-issue cabinets and shelves. Instead outfit your bath with amenities that are as much about enhancing the look of the room as they are about organizing bath accoutrements.

1. A modest-size makeup counter takes advantage of the storage and counterspace that custom cabinetry provides.

2. These stacked cubes of walnut, maple, and painted wood pivot on a lazy Susan base for easy access to stored items.

3. Borrowing a trend from lavish hotels, a wallmount rack stacks folded towels within the tub alcove. Hooks beneath the shelf hang wet towels to dry.

4. This multipurpose chrome pole system offers flexible storage. A variety of swiveling shelves and rods or rings (for towels) is available. A cosmetic mirror fits anywhere in between. The pole attachments adjust to desired heights.

5. Pullout towel storage makes the most of a narrow space and serves as a transition between the vanity and makeup areas.

6. Recessed niches in this marble shower wall contain bathtime accessories without taking up any floor space.

3

4

5

6

Skylights and an elaborate dormer keep the mood light and bright despite a dark-stain vanity.

CHAPTER 8

Lighting & Comfort Systems

Devise a Lighting Plan, Lighting Fixtures, Windows and Skylights, Heating and Ventilation

You may take it for granted, but proper lighting can make or break a bath design. Lighting helps you clearly see the mirror when you're grooming, ensures you can see where items are for safety's sake, and sets the mood for the beautiful bath you've put together. Shadowless, glare-free illumination is paramount to close work, such as plucking brows or removing splinters. In addition to ambient and task lighting, natural light from skylights and windows makes your bath more inviting. For a comfortable space, the right heating and ventilation elements are also a must. Ventilation from open windows and fans is necessary for keeping what could be a damp environment dry and welcoming. And supplemental heat sources such as towel warmers and radiant-heat flooring ensure that your bath is cozy and comfortable year-round.

An elegant soaking tub basks in a sunny alcove. The heated towel bar delivers warm after-bath wraps.

DEVISE A LIGHTING PLAN

In a properly lighted bath, shadowless, glare-free illumination is the rule. Plan to use more than one type of lighting. Ambient and task lighting work well together. Accent lighting has a place in many baths as well. Provide separate controls for each mode.

Ambient, or general, lighting creates uniform, overall glow in the entire bath space and comes from one or more sources, usually overhead. (If your bath is larger than 35 square feet, one overhead fixture will not be enough.) Backing up this general lighting plan is task lighting. These fixtures eliminate shadows in the areas where you perform specific tasks, such as applying makeup, shaving, or taking a bath. Accent lighting occurs when you aim light on an object or surface simply to show it off. For this job you'll need a lightbulb or lamp with a beam that is three to five times brighter than the general lighting lamps. Learn more about lightbulbs on page 177.

Lighting the mirror

Your bathroom mirror serves as the primary grooming center in the house, so you want to make sure it is evenly illuminated and free of shadows. To do this, light sources must be evenly distributed from above, below, and both sides. This cross-lighting technique prevents shadows that hinder makeup application.

Plan to install one or two fixtures above the mirror to cast light just over the front edge of the sink and countertop. Then put a light on each side of the mirror, centered at eye level. If there is no space for such side fixtures, you can make the light above the mirror longer than the width of the mirror itself. To take advantage of the reflection, choose a light color countertop (preferably white).

No matter your approach to mirror lighting, select bulbs designed for vanity illumination. These bulbs generate light in the daylight spectrum. Avoid choosing bulbs that are too white or too yellow. They won't reflect a true picture of how you look outside of the bathroom.

Mirror, Mirror

Mirrors perform multiple functions and require only an expanse of wall space. A mirror's size, shape, and frame contribute to the bathroom's ambience. In addition to providing a spot for checking your appearance, mirrors extend and reinforce the lighting and general tone of your bathroom. They help reflect and redistribute light throughout the room, whether it's sunlight streaming in through windows or general lighting from artificial sources. Mirrors can help add depth too, so a small bath appears much larger than it really is.

Light fixtures above mirrors are musts for grooming areas. The plain mirrors above these dual pedestal sinks are framed with limestone tile used elsewhere in the room.

Shower and tub lighting

In an enclosed shower or tub most building codes require enclosed vaporproof downlights. Place the fixtures so that they fully light the tub or shower but don't shine directly in your eyes when you're relaxing in the tub. One centrally located fixture, installed in the ceiling or high on the wall, should be enough to adequately light a shower stall. Locate light switches at least 6 feet from a tub or shower.

A trio of sconces provides illumination at this double vanity, while the framed mirrors add a touch of elegance.

Elegant light fixtures—including new sconces based on a 1930s design and a 1940s Murano glass chandelier—orchestrate a glamorous yet functional aesthetic in this bath.

LIGHTING FIXTURES

Scores of light fixtures await your selection. You will likely find several types to fully light your bath.

Recessed downlights. Also called can lights, these are very popular and are the least obtrusive fixtures for general or task lighting. For the best ambient lighting, position them close enough together for their light patterns to overlap.

Pendant lights. Lights that hang from a wire, rod, or chain work well in the bathroom, either as overall ambient light or as task lighting over the vanity. If you have a large traditional-style bath, a small chandelier promotes the look and feel of a living space rather than a utilitarian room.

Surface-mount fixtures. These fixtures work well in bathrooms that cannot accommodate recessed fixtures, a common problem in bath remodeling. Available in many styles and sizes, surface-mount fixtures accommodate both incandescent and fluorescent bulbs.

Wall sconces. For ambient lighting, use wall sconces throughout the bath. Wall sconces placed on each side of a mirror offer shadow-free task light for applying makeup and shaving.

Shower fixtures. For safety, shower fixtures must be waterproof and steamproof; most building codes require this.

Dimmers. These light-regulating knobs, switches, and levers enable you to set the fixture at any level of light from a soft glow to radiant brightness. In this way they save energy because you use just the amount of light you need.

Bulb Basics

Lightbulb options extend far beyond one-size-fits-all incandescent bulbs.

Incandescent. Thomas Edison introduced them in 1879 and they are still widely used and appreciated for their white light. Low-voltage incandescent fixtures make good accent lights. Operating on 12 or 24 volts, they require transformers that are sometimes built into the fixture.

Fluorescent. Compact fluorescent lamps (CFLs) fit any fixture that takes incandescent bulbs. They offer much greater energy efficiency and longer life than incandescents. Their light quality is equivalent to that of incandescents, although some brands still take about a minute to reach full brightness. You'll also find fluorescent circles and rope lights for cabinet and cove lighting.

Halogen. Quartz halogen lights offer bright white light good for task or accent lighting. Usually low-voltage these bulbs do put off a small amount of heat. Choose a fixture specifically designed for halogen bulbs.

A halogen sconce with multicolor accents is a point of interest and an option for task lighting near the vanity.

WINDOWS AND SKYLIGHTS

Proper lighting goes beyond choosing the right fixtures. A good plan includes as much natural light as possible, putting windows, skylights, glass doors, wall cutouts, and glass block to work. Mirrors, too, play a part, reflecting and increasing the amount of natural light that enters your bath.

Windows

Window selection and placement, in particular, are key to creating a visually pleasing bath with adequate ventilation.

Think inside and outside: Look for places to install additional windows where they will shed more light on the vanity without looking out of place on your home's exterior. Consider installing a frosted-glass door or an open cutout between the master bath and bedroom to increase the light flow from one room into the other.

Let your room's proportions and features dictate window size. Windows intended to accent a tub, for example, look best when they match the tub's length or width. To maximize airflow, place two or more operable windows on opposite or adjacent walls. Windows placed high on a wall introduce light without compromising privacy. If views warrant attention and your home is secluded, you can enjoy the surroundings while you indulge in a soothing bath.

Skylights

If wall space is limited or views are less than appealing, a skylight may be the answer. Operable models, called sky windows, offer ventilation as well as light and have frames that match wall windows. Skylights offer an ideal way to bring daylight into a bath, providing your bath's location allows for it. To prevent moisture and condensation problems, choose a high-quality model and install it according to the manufacturer's specifications.

A second-story venue grants the opportunity for a bath surrounded by trees, making it a striking spot for a relaxing soak.

A massive mirror built into the wall reflects light and views from the windows, brightening the space and making it seem larger. The clear glass shower enclosure furthers the sense of openness.

A row of skylights is a welcome wake-up call and a good way to let in natural light while preserving wall space for fixtures and other functional items.

Operable windows are a good source of
ventilation and cooling breezes.

HEATING AND VENTILATION

Without proper ventilation the ceiling may mildew, the wallpaper may curl, the paint may peel, and the mirror may begin to deteriorate. Open windows when you can and supplement them with a high-quality ventilation fan.

Ventilation

Ventilation fans aren't often thought of as safety devices, but by exhausting warm, moist air, they reduce the likelihood that mold and mildew will develop in the bathroom. Proper use dictates that the fan is on whenever the shower is on. For maximum benefit the fan should run for 15 to 20 minutes after showering ends. One way to help "forgetful" family members is to install a timer switch that turns off the fan after a set period. Even better, consider a fan control with a humidity sensor that turns the unit on and off automatically.

Choosing an Exhaust Fan

Ventilation keeps it cool and clean. Beyond that comfort factor many building codes require exhaust fans in new baths. Three criteria matter when choosing a ventilation fan:

How much air the fan moves. A vent fan should move the air in the bathroom from inside to out eight times an hour. To determine the size you need, measure your bath's cubic feet (width times length times ceiling height) and multiply the result by 8, then divide by 60. The result is the minimum cubic feet per minute (cfm) rating you'll need in a venting fan. A 100-square-foot bath needs a fan rated at 105 cfm or higher. Take into account the size of the room and number and placement of windows.

How much noise the fan makes. The noise from a fan will resonate on the hard surfaces of a bathroom, so choose a quiet fan that vents to the outside. Sound is rated in sones; a higher rating means the fan is louder. Look for fans with a noise level not exceeding 3 sones; anything less than 2 sones is highly recommended.

How the vent looks. Once size, efficiency, and sound are considered, choose a vent style that matches the rest of the room.

A fireplace built into the wall is a picturesque amenity. The fireplace has a gas inset for ease of use and low maintenance.

Heating

Extra heat sources can make spending time in the bathroom more comfortable. Mount electric heaters on walls, in the ceiling, or under toe-kicks to warm specific areas of the room; models are available for use with gas or propane as well. Another option is radiant heat, installed beneath the floor to warm bare feet. (Learn more about radiant-heat flooring on page 98.) Spot sources, such as infrared heat lamps and electric or hydronic towel warmers, take the chill out of drying off.

Fireplaces

Soaking in a tub in front of the fireplace is no longer a luxury reserved only for trips to the spa. A fireplace radiates tranquility as well as warmth. Fireplaces are often installed in a wall between the bedroom and bathroom so both spaces benefit. Another option is to build a fireplace in a corner of the room. Woodburning fireplaces are less common than gas or electric models. Regardless of type the placement of the fireplace is a priority and must be determined early. Installation is best handled by an expert who can ensure that proper ventilation and safety precautions are taken.

DESIGN GALLERY
Spa Touches

Who needs a trip to the spa when your own bath boasts plush towels, elegant furnishings, and other quintessentially spalike elements? This kind of luxury is worth escaping to anytime.

1. With comfortable furnishings such as this armchair, the bathroom becomes a haven for relaxation.

2. Little details—an ottoman, a tray of candles, a spray of favorite flowers, and thick towels—add comforting touches.

3. A beverage center with a small sink and refrigerator provides refreshments for a master suite. Outfit yours with a coffeemaker for a morning latte.

4. A polished-chrome warmer keeps towels toasty.

5. Multiple showerheads and body sprays make any bathroom more spalike.

6. A radiant-heat floor and gas fireplace ensure a warm experience in this bath.

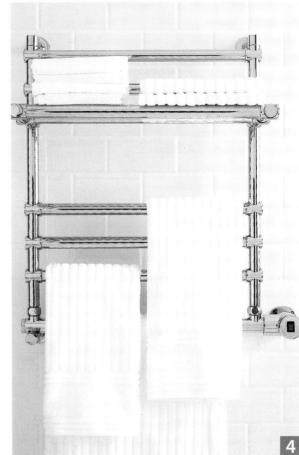

The polished look of this bath is the outcome of careful planning, consulting with bath design professionals, and clear communication with contractors.

CHAPTER 9

Realize Your Dreams

Survive the Remodeling Process, Professionals,
Hiring a Contractor, Bids, Estimates, Contracts,
DIY Considerations, Stages and Timelines,
Codes and Permits, Planning Kit

You're on the brink of the actual remodeling work, which means you're about to begin the most exciting and the messiest part of the project. First you need to gather cost estimates and decide who will do the work. If you've drawn the floor plans yourself, have your ideas reviewed by design professionals, who can help refine and improve them as necessary. If you plan to hire a contractor, use the advice in this chapter to obtain bids and sort through estimates. This preliminary work is your ticket to enjoying the remodeling journey that takes you to the completion of your new bathroom.

Finishing details often are the result of working with a qualified design professional. A homeowner may not have thought to include a graceful curve in the marble backsplash, for instance.

SURVIVE THE REMODELING PROCESS

The mess and inconvenience of living in your home while the bathroom is renovated is easier to handle if you're prepared. Living without a functioning toilet or sink is inconvenient at best. It's important to coordinate with your contractor to minimize the time the bathroom is out of service and to plan family schedules so you're out of the house when it's not functioning. Have a set plan before the work begins to minimize disruption.

Stay on schedule
Unless your project is very simple, you may appreciate the expertise of a general contractor who will schedule professional subcontractors and keep the renovation on track. The general contractor knows the best order to complete each aspect of the work so the whole project will take the least time to complete. (See pages 190–191 for information about hiring contractors.)

Control dust
Most contractors, at minimum, tape a plastic barrier at doorways to reduce the amount of dust that escapes from the construction zone. Some may also tape off heat registers and change the furnace filters daily, especially when sanding drywall. Request that they cover the walkways and carpeted areas that lead to the bathroom with drop cloths.

Keep reasonable hours
Ask workers to arrive and leave at reasonable hours for your household. Understand that if you set shorter workdays, the project may take longer. Noise during the work hours is out of your control, but you can let the contractor know in advance if there are times when your house is off-limits.

Protect children
Kids and construction sites are a bad mix. Power tools, exposed wires, open stairwells, and building materials can lead to a trip to the emergency room. When possible keep the door to the work area shut and locked. When that's not possible, divert the kids with a trip to Grandma's (or a friend's) house.

A major remodel—like the one that created this stunning master bath—can disrupt your home life for a long time. Smart scheduling makes the intrusion easier to handle.

An architect can help you achieve a well-integrated design. Woodwork and materials help tie this Asian-inspired suite to the traditional style of the house.

PROFESSIONALS

Unless your bath project entails a simple facelift or you have considerable design experience, you may wish to enlist a handful of professionals, such as an architect, NKBA-certified bath designer, interior designer, or a member of a design/build team. A professional can help you express your thoughts on paper as well as offer fresh ideas. Equally important, the experience and expertise of professionals ensure that the project will meet local building codes and they'll likely help you avoid expensive mistakes.

Architects

Working primarily with the structure and organization of space, architects are familiar with many types of building materials, finishes, and appliances and have thorough knowledge of structural, electrical, plumbing, heating, ventilation, and air-conditioning systems. Have an architect or structural engineer prepare plans that include structural changes to your house and those that the local building and planning commission will review. Depending on the project and the work, architects may charge a percentage of the project's total cost, an hourly rate, or a flat fee that you both agree on at the beginning of the project.

NKBA-certified designers

Professionals with this certification have passed NKBA examinations, have extensive industry experience, and meet NKBA continuing education requirements. What does it mean to you? It's another level of assurance that you're hiring a professional who has the knowledge and experience necessary to get your job done right. Because these professionals specialize in bath and kitchen design, they are likely to have deeper knowledge of the specifics of bathroom design than a more general design professional who works on a variety of residential projects.

Interior designers

Need help creating an interior space that meets your functional and aesthetic goals? An interior designer is the person to hire. Traditionally interior designers work with colors, wall finishes, fabrics, floor coverings, furnishings, lighting, and accessories to personalize a space. Those who are certified by the American Society of Interior Designers (ASID), however, must also demonstrate an ongoing knowledge of materials, government regulations, safety standards, and the latest products. These designers generally are familiar with building codes and structural requirements and can make recommendations for placement of partition walls, plumbing hookups, electrical outlets, and architectural details such as built-in storage units, moldings, door styles and sizes, and windows.

Design/build teams

For complete project management from initial design to completion of construction, enlist the help of a design/build team. Involvement from the beginning of the project ensures that team members are thoroughly familiar with the building methods and techniques specified by the project plan. If design/build teams don't offer the services of a registered architect, structural modifications will require the approval of an architect or structural engineer.

Locate a Design Professional

To find a design professional, refer to your phone book or search the websites of the National Kitchen and Bath Association (nkba.org), American Institute of Architects (aia.org) or the American Society of Interior Designers (asid.org).

Although the National Association of Home Builders (NAHB) does not have a national certification program, many states have certification programs for builders and remodelers. In addition the National Association of the Remodeling Industry (NARI) has a Certified Remodeling Professionals program. To find a NARI-certified remodeler or NARI member, use the search engine at nari.org.

HIRING A CONTRACTOR

Unless you have plenty of time to devote to your bath project and are an accomplished do-it-yourselfer, you'll probably want to hire a professional building contractor. Take the time necessary to choose a contractor who has a good reputation and with whom you feel comfortable.

A licensed contractor has completed state requirements to perform various types of work. General contractors usually have a broad knowledge of all aspects of construction and are hired to organize and complete a job according to an agreed-on schedule. Specialized contractors, such as electrical contractors, are called subcontractors. Electrical contractors, for example, have passed state certification programs that permit them to perform work relating to

electrical hookups. It is the responsibility of your general contractor to hire the subcontractors necessary for the completion of your project.

To find a qualified general contractor:

Ask friends, neighbors, or colleagues for the names of reliable contractors they have hired. Get several recommendations.

Meet with prospective contractors to discuss your project. Ask about their experience with bathroom projects as well as problems they have encountered in the past. Ask for a ballpark figure for the project. This won't be a precise bid and you shouldn't regard it as an agreement. However discussing money at an early stage may give you an idea of how knowledgeable a contractor is and how comfortable he or she is with discussing costs.

Ask how long they have been in business and whether they carry insurance. Without insurance you're liable for accidents that occur on your property. Contractors must have a certificate of insurance to cover damage, liability, and workers' compensation. It is acceptable to ask to see the certification before proceeding.

Obtain references from contractors and take the time to inspect their work. Reliable contractors provide this information readily and are proud to display their work. Run their names by the Better Business Bureau to see if any unresolved complaints are on file.

Narrow your choices to three to five contractors and ask for final bids. (See pages 193–195.) Give the contractors the same deadline for submitting bids—about three weeks should be sufficient. Eliminate from contention any contractor who posts a late bid; having too much work is not a valid excuse.

Review each bid carefully to see how thoroughly they have been researched. The bid should include an amount specified for the contractor's fee, usually 10 to 15 percent of the total costs.

Custom shower enclosures such as this two-person one featuring glass mosaic tile and sleek controls set high to accommodate the tall homeowner are best left to building and remodeling professionals.

Take all factors into account, including price, when making the final selection of your general contractor. Be skeptical of any bid that is significantly lower than the others. The lowest bidder may not deliver the most satisfying results.

Make an ongoing effort to keep lines of communication open once you hire your contractor. Schedule regular meetings to discuss progress and keep informed of interim deadlines. Tell your contractor that you don't expect to make your final payment until the job has passed required building inspections, you have seen written proof that subcontractors and suppliers have been paid, and you and your contractor have walked through the project and agreed that it is complete.

This tempting bath retreat showcases the work of custom cabinet makers, decorative painters, and certified bath designers. Careful attention to every detail—including jets set low in the whirlpool so they go unseen—is key.

Working with a Contractor

A good working relationship will achieve the best results. Keep these tips in mind for the smoothest path to finishing your bath project.

Frequent check-ins. While it's unrealistic to plan your schedule around the contractor's, try to coordinate a time when he or she can discuss progress. That way you can quickly assess the work done the previous day and discuss any problems or upcoming decisions. Once you've met for a few minutes, avoid hovering—it will slow the work pace.

Open communication. Speak up immediately if you are displeased. The longer you wait the more expensive and difficult corrections will be. Be clear about what you would rather see and use a polite tone. Remember to express what you're pleased with as the project moves along.

Obviously you are hiring a contractor to do good work, but compliments can go a long way toward getting top-notch results.

Changes in writing. Though you want to minimize changes—they generally are costly—you may need to alter plans after work has started. Put any "change" agreements in writing, and make them as precise and detailed as the original contract.

Financial updates. Before the project starts decide with your contractor how often you'll discuss money. Frequent checkpoints will allow you both to assess whether the project is on budget. No matter how detailed your contract, setbacks beyond your control can occur. Be prepared to discuss how problems may affect the budget and how to adjust the plan to keep costs down.

When writing a contract be sure to specify which work you're hiring contractors to do and what you plan to do yourself. If you have a modest budget but want to splurge on specialized details like this tub alcove, you may wish to paint the walls or handle the decorating.

BIDS, ESTIMATES, CONTRACTS

Once you have narrowed your list of prospective contractors, it's time to get final bids from each. If you hire a general contractor, that person will need to get bids from subcontractors. In either case it's your responsibility to ensure that you get a carefully prepared bid for the clearly defined project you want completed. Follow these guidelines for obtaining bids, preparing estimates, and making contracts to be sure you find a contractor who fits your budget and gets the job done right.

Obtaining bids

The bidding process is the same whether you're gathering bids on a complete project from a general contractor or a portion of the work from a subcontractor. Request bids based on your plans from the list of contractors you have selected. If you want to include specific fixtures or features in your project, list them and give the list to the bidding contractors. Three weeks is a reasonable amount of time

Review the estimate and check allowances for specific items such as this faucet. Compare the estimates with actual costs of quality products in the styles you like.

for each of them to provide a bid. When bids return expect specific, itemized materials lists; a schedule noting what will be done when and when payments will be made based on that progress; and the contractor's fee. Bid prices are not necessarily predictors of the quality of work or materials to be used so ask contractors to explain their bids in detail.

Preparing estimates

If you'll be doing most of the work, determine costs by breaking work into manageable chunks. Rather than shopping at several stores for the best prices on individual items, find one home center and lumber source that offers reasonable prices and top-notch service and use it for everything. Save time and avoid hassles by getting to know the staff at the store you choose. Visit when the store isn't busy and share your plans with the staff. A good salesperson can become a valuable adviser at this stage of your project.

Comparing Bids

When it's time to evaluate bids and choose a contractor, make sure to:

Check that each contractor has the same information. Otherwise you can expect prices to vary because components won't be consistent with all the bids.

Compare line items from bid to bid. One contractor's estimate for materials may be less than another's because he or she bid lower-quality materials. Consider what is more important to you—budget or quality—before selecting.

Be wary of extremely low bids. The bid could be low because it doesn't include all aspects of the job such as removal of waste from the site.

Base your decision on more than the final cost. Compare the estimated time frame between bids—higher costs are justified if the work is being done on a faster schedule. Be sure to check references from each contractor and factor that into your final decision as well.

Ask the contractor to clarify or further explain if you don't understand an estimate on the bid. It's better to know and understand all the information before making your decision.

Making a contract

Select a contractor and sign a written contract. Many contractors have prepared forms. If you are unsure about the specific points of a contract, consult a lawyer before signing. A good contract should cover these points:

- A precise description of all work to be completed by the contractor and subcontractors and work to be done by you.
- A detailed description of materials to be installed, including specific types and brands of fixtures, materials, and finishes.
- The total cost of the job, including all materials, labor, and fees.
- A schedule of payments that you will make to the contractor. Be wary of contracts that ask for large payments up front—some states even limit the allowable amount made to contractors before work begins. The schedule of payments should coordinate with dates specified for completion of each stage of the project.
- A work schedule with calendar dates specified for completion of each stage of the project. The schedule should include an allowance for delays resulting from delivery problems, weather-related interruptions (if applicable), and back orders of scarce products.
- A "right of rescission" that allows homeowners to back out of the contract within 72 hours of signing.
- A certificate of insurance that guarantees the contractor has the appropriate insurance.
- A warranty that guarantees that the labor and materials are free from defects for a certain period of time (usually one year).
- An arbitration clause that specifies the precise method you will use to settle disputes.
- A description of change-order procedures stating what will happen if you decide to alter the plans or specifications after the contract has been signed. The description should include a fee structure for change requests.
- A release of liens to ensure that the homeowners won't incur liens or charges against the property as a result of legal actions filed against the contractor or any of the subcontractors hired.

A general contractor and professional subcontractors have the expertise to make informed decisions about everything from flooring to fixtures.

Design Tip

No matter how carefully bids are prepared, savvy homeowners know that a remodeling project usually ends up costing 10 to 15 percent more than estimated. Unexpected problems and changes often occur. After hammers start swinging, enthusiastic homeowners often upgrade plans and materials, figuring that "as long as we've gone to this much trouble, let's go further." Spare yourself hassle and headache: Anticipate budget overruns.

Hiring the right contractor ensures that all elements of your bathroom design—from the installation of sinks, faucets, and countertops to the placement of lighting and towel bars—are completed successfully.

DIY CONSIDERATIONS

Hiring a general contractor to complete your entire bathroom project is a comprehensive approach to getting your renovation completed. But it's not the only option. You may choose to do some or all of the project yourself depending on your skills, time, physical abilities, and budget. It pays to consider these alternatives to hiring a general contractor before you begin.

Do most of it yourself

If you have the tools, skills, time, inclination, energy, and physical ability, you can save a lot of money by doing much of the work. Before you tear into a big project, however, do an honest self-assessment. Total the cost of tools you'll have to buy or rent to get the project done (if any). Account for the time it will take you to order and pick up materials

and learn necessary techniques. If you plan to take time off from work to complete the project, count the cost of lost earnings. Then consider the cost (in time and money) of a potential mistake. Miscutting a piece of drywall may cost a few dollars in wasted material and a few minutes of time (if you've purchased an extra sheet or two for such a situation), but miscutting a piece of expensive flooring will cost a lot more. Wrestling with heavy materials and large fixtures, or trying to work long hours to maintain a schedule can result in injury, an even greater cost. It may be cheaper and less risky to hire out some jobs, such as installing a large tub, tiling a custom shower surround, or completing extensive wiring or plumbing modifications. Hiring out allows you to concentrate on jobs that better suit your skills, physical condition, confidence level, and available tools.

Tackle some of it yourself

You may choose to do a portion of the work and hire out the rest. One way is to act as general contractor; the other is to hire a general contractor. Either way pencil yourself in as the responsible party for the tasks you want to complete. Here are some strategies for sorting out who does what:

Manage the materials. Order, purchase, and arrange the delivery of supplies.

Be a laborer. Do work that requires more labor than materials and skill, such as demolition, painting, and cleanup.

Do the costly work. If you have the skills and tools and if code allows, tackle the plumbing or electrical tasks and leave less specialized—and less expensive—efforts to others.

Be an apprentice. Ask your contractor to leave minor jobs, such as daily cleanup, for you to do.

Replacing an existing faucet is within the skill level of most do-it-yourselfers. This stainless-steel faucet complements a contemporary bath. A coating of marine varnish protects the ebony backsplash.

Be your own general contractor

If your skills are more administrative than technical, filling the role of general contractor can be a source of pride. Be aware that this job is also extremely time-consuming and challenging. As a general contractor you manage the purchase and delivery of materials, hire subcontractors, communicate plans to each, coordinate work schedules and inspections, and pay everyone. You'll have to select subcontractors carefully. Most subcontractors favor professional contractors over armchair generals because professionals are often a steady source of income. Before making the decision to be your own general contractor, talk to other people who have done it and find out what lessons and advice they have to offer. Also check local libraries and websites for further information.

If you have the tools, the time, and the skills, you may be able to finish at least some of your bathroom yourself, particularly if the project is a facelift or renovation for which existing plumbing and electrical systems will stay in place.

DIY Ideas

Even homeowners with generous budgets sometimes like to roll up their sleeves and get to work. Trouble is most don't have time to do all of the hands-on work, and some tasks require tools and skills that are anything but ordinary. When sweat equity makes sense, by all means dig in, but leave more complicated projects to experienced tradespeople. A do-it-yourselfer might paint, install moldings, lay ceramic tile, install a faucet, wallpaper, and do light demolition. Other tasks amateurs can handle include:

Simple framing. Home improvement guidebooks can help, so simple jobs, such as framing a partition wall, lie within reach of do-it-yourselfers. Existing electrical or plumbing systems complicate matters—training is required in such cases.

Drywall. Hanging and taping drywall is a relatively simple task—if you can measure accurately—though it is time-consuming and a little tedious. You can fasten drywall with special cup-head nails, but driving drywall screws with a portable or cordless drill yields better long-term results and allows you to shift or remove and reinstall panels (before taping) without damaging them.

Cabinet installation. Although it takes a serious investment in equipment and training to build custom cabinets, installing stock cabinetry requires fewer tools and skills. Most manufacturers anticipate the likelihood of DIY remodeling and package installation instructions with the cabinets.

STAGES AND TIMELINES

It's difficult to come up with a general timeline for all bathroom projects because each will vary depending on size, available funding, and the amount of work being done—ranging from a simple facelift to a complex addition. The timeline here is meant only to provide an idea of how much time the initial steps leading to the remodeling work may take as well as to help you keep track of the steps involved in the actual project.

The homeowners selected elements that make this bathroom an intimate refuge—such as the nature-inspired leaf and vine wallpaper and creamy tile—early in the process to achieve a cohesive finished bath.

PROJECT TIMELINE

Step 1 (4 weeks) Preplanning*
- ❏ Collect ideas
- ❏ Assess your space
- ❏ Identify major problems
- ❏ Develop a budget
- ❏ Identify financing options
- ❏ Identify possible contractors

Step 2 (4–8 weeks) Selection of Professionals
- ❏ Request bids from contractors
- ❏ Determine financing
- ❏ Select and hire a contractor

Step 3 (2–6 weeks) Design Development
- ❏ Learn building code requirements
- ❏ Create a rough plan
- ❏ Discuss and refine plan with an architect or building designer
- ❏ Approve design plan and sign design agreement

Step 4 (2–4 weeks) Preconstruction
- ❏ Select products
- ❏ Obtain permits
- ❏ Prepare calendar of work, material ordering, and inspections
- ❏ Order materials
- ❏ Prepare home for construction

Step 5 (2–8 weeks) Construction
- ❏ Complete demolition if necessary
- ❏ Begin major structural and mechanical work
- ❏ Frame partitions and walls if necessary
- ❏ Install plumbing, wiring, and other internal systems
- ❏ Install fixtures
- ❏ Install flooring
- ❏ Install cabinetry
- ❏ Apply wall and ceiling surface finishes
- ❏ Do any additional finishing

Step 6 (1–3 weeks) Final Steps
- ❏ Inspect the job
- ❏ Ensure everything is to code
- ❏ Obtain the final inspection certificate
- ❏ Make any final payments for materials or services
- ❏ Accessorize and enjoy your new bathroom

*The preplanning stage takes an estimated four weeks. For some people, however, this step alone might take a year or more to complete. Many homeowners begin collecting bathroom ideas years before they consider undertaking a remodeling project. Only you can know when the timing is right to move past the initial idea phase of the project.

Completely renovating the bathroom in a 1930s-era home resulted in this contemporary open design. Typically a lengthy timeline precedes the completion of a full-scale project.

Building codes require GFCI receptacles, lights, and switches in the bathroom to reduce the risk of electrical shock. Additional codes may regulate outward swinging doors, such as the one here, which accesses a veranda.

CODES AND PERMITS

Building codes are specifically designed to protect the structural integrity of your home and remove potential threats to your health and safety. Many codes vary from place to place, but the good news is you don't have to learn every detail of local codes to plan a bathroom renovation. Your local building official is there to help you achieve what you want from the project and obtain a building permit.

For your first visit with the building official, be prepared to describe your project—even if your ideas are rough—and ask what building codes apply. Bring a rough sketch of the bathroom, as well as the location and dimensions of the windows and doors, to make your visit even more productive. Don't be discouraged if local codes call for a standard that you don't think you can meet. If safety or practicality isn't compromised, building officials may be willing to make exceptions to accommodate existing homes.

Codes to consider

Codes govern many safety elements. For instance, building codes require that you use GFCI receptacles in a bathroom. These outlets sense shock hazards and shut off a receptacle or circuit if necessary. If lights will be installed in a shower or tub enclosure, most building codes require enclosed, vapor-proof downlights. Building codes also govern construction, including materials for fire safety, lumber specifications, stud and joist spacing, and nail and screw types and spacing. Code typically also governs mechanicals. These may include electric cable type, number and placement of receptacles, GFCIs, and plumbing pipe material (copper, plastic, steel), size, solder type, venting, traps, and connections.

Permits

Remember to contact your local municipality and county building departments to see what permits are required for your project. In some areas you may need a separate permit for each stage of your project. If your plans are limited to changing surface materials you probably won't need a permit. But if you'll be making changes to your home's plumbing or electrical systems, you'll probably need at least one.

Common inspections

Because the scope of bathroom projects varies dramatically, the actual inspections required for your project, if any, will depend on the specific components of your project. Some of these—such as a roofing inspection—may be necessary only if you have built an addition. Other inspections are required for any renovation more extensive than a simple surface facelift. Check with your local building official before work begins so you can be sure all necessary inspections occur at the proper stages of your project.

Most building codes require sufficient ventilation in a bathroom. Operable windows are one means of achieving this, but an exhaust fan is convenient during the cold months. It's best to have both.

PLANNING KIT

To transform your bath dreams into a reality, you must consider the details. Sketch ideas of your own with the planning kit on this and the following pages—it will come in handy even if you work with a design professional later on.

Plot the space

Use a photocopier to reproduce the planning grid on page 205 at its original size then use a crafts knife or scissors to copy and cut out the templates on pages 203–204. One square on the grid equals 1 square foot of floor space. The templates include plan-view (top-down) perspectives. Plot the entire bathroom, including any closets and interior full and partial walls you'd like to build. If your new bathroom will include a dressing area, breakfast bar, or other new adjacent spaces, plot those as well.

Visualize how the room's various zones—washing, bathing, toilet, storage, and perhaps sitting, exercising, or snacking—relate to one another. Figure out where you'd like these various zones to go and how they best fit into the available floor space. Consider how the bath relates to the surrounding rooms such as bedrooms, walk-in closets, dressing rooms, halls, or sitting rooms. Plan, too, what architectural features you'd like to add or highlight and which types, sizes, and styles of fixtures, cabinetry, shelving, and furniture you want to include.

One of the keys to making the bath functional and beautiful is good placement (the placement of doors, windows, fixtures, cabinetry, and built-in features such as shelving or towel warmers). Use the provided symbols to position existing architectural features. Use a different color to indicate features such as built-ins and freestanding furniture that you plan to include. If you have furniture or special features that aren't part of the templates, draw them to scale on the grid paper. Mark obstructions, including prominent light fixtures and angled ceilings, with dotted lines. Pay attention to details such as door swings and drawer extensions as you consider the placement of these items. If you're building a new addition, mark the existing structure in one color and use a different one to mark the addition.

See pages 112–113 for information on floor plans.

Design Tip

Computer software programs enable homeowners to develop two- and three-dimensional floor plans for the bath. Some programs let you add color, and even texture, to each surface. These design tools are invaluable to those who have trouble visualizing how a flat floor plan will translate into a three-dimensional space. This planning kit is a more basic option though equally useful. Just make a photocopy of the grid paper then trace or photocopy the templates to arrange and rearrange the elements within the footprint.

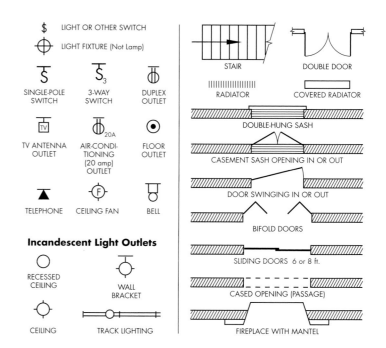

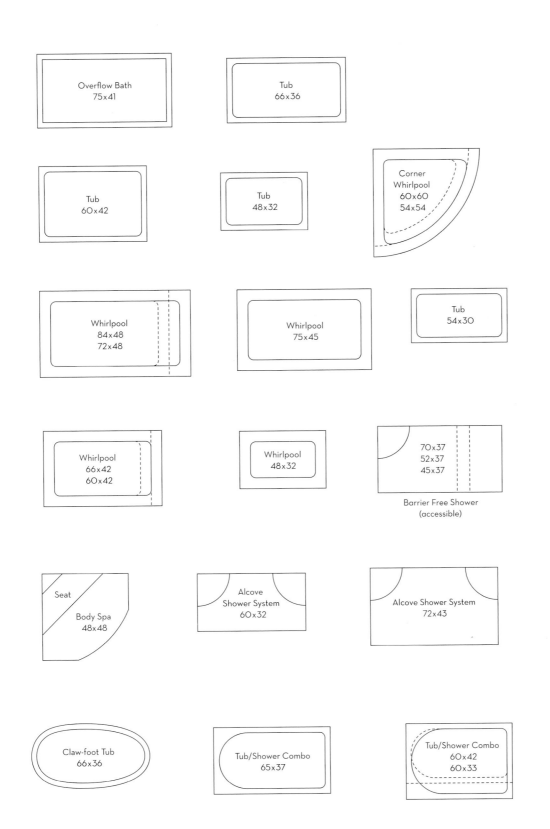

Overflow Bath
75x41

Tub
66x36

Tub
60x42

Tub
48x32

Corner
Whirlpool
60x60
54x54

Whirlpool
84x48
72x48

Whirlpool
75x45

Tub
54x30

Whirlpool
66x42
60x42

Whirlpool
48x32

70x37
52x37
45x37

Barrier Free Shower
(accessible)

Seat

Body Spa
48x48

Alcove
Shower System
60x32

Alcove Shower System
72x43

Claw-foot Tub
66x36

Tub/Shower Combo
65x37

Tub/Shower Combo
60x42
60x33

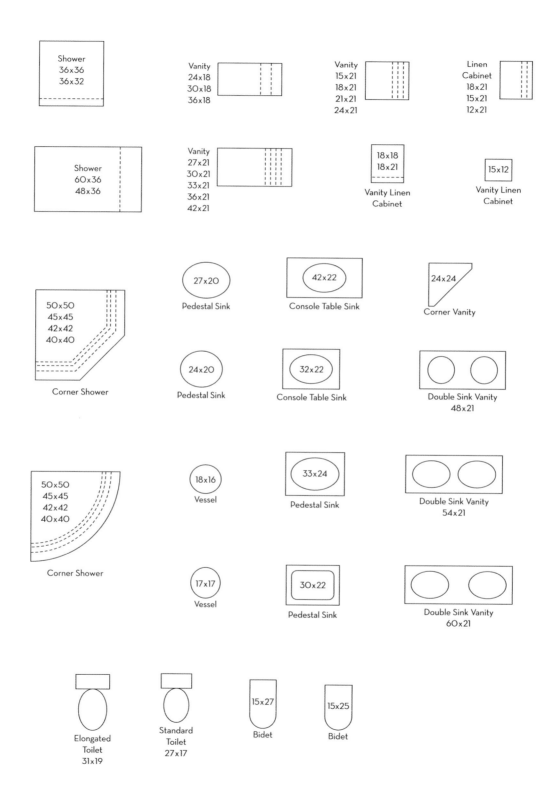

Shower
36x36
36x32

Vanity
24x18
30x18
36x18

Vanity
15x21
18x21
21x21
24x21

Linen
Cabinet
18x21
15x21
12x21

Shower
60x36
48x36

Vanity
27x21
30x21
33x21
36x21
42x21

18x18
18x21
Vanity Linen
Cabinet

15x12
Vanity Linen
Cabinet

50x50
45x45
42x42
40x40
Corner Shower

27x20
Pedestal Sink

42x22
Console Table Sink

24x24
Corner Vanity

24x20
Pedestal Sink

32x22
Console Table Sink

Double Sink Vanity
48x21

50x50
45x45
42x42
40x40
Corner Shower

18x16
Vessel

33x24
Pedestal Sink

Double Sink Vanity
54x21

17x17
Vessel

30x22
Pedestal Sink

Double Sink Vanity
60x21

Elongated
Toilet
31x19

Standard
Toilet
27x17

15x27
Bidet

15x25
Bidet

Bath remodeling is a lot of hard work, but it pays off in a job done right. This finished master bath succeeds with tranquil colors and soothing textures.

CHAPTER 10

Resources

Resource Guide, Glossary, Index

The job of planning and finishing a bathroom that meets your needs and desires requires a lot of work and what can seem, at times, to be endless decision-making. Depending on how extensive your project will be, you may want to involve professionals in some or all phases of it. Names and contact information for some of the many associations and organizations involved in residential remodel projects are found on the following pages. Turn to these groups and local resources for assistance. This chapter also includes a list of terms common to remodeling and bath projects. Though you don't need to be an expert in the terminology, familiarity with these words and their meanings may result in more productive conversations with professionals.

If you hit a bump in your plans and can't figure out what to do, several national remodeling and building organizations offer assistance. Contact them to help your dream of a beautiful bath like this one become a reality.

RESOURCE GUIDE

Remodeling Resources

American Homeowners Foundation
6776 Little Falls Rd.
Arlington, VA 22213
800/489-7776
americanhomeowners.org

American Institute of Architects
1735 New York Ave. NW
Washington, DC 20006
202/626-7300
800/242-3837 aia.org

American Society
of Interior Designers
608 Massachusetts Ave. NE
Washington, DC 20002
202/546-3480 asid.org

ENERGY STAR
U.S. Environmental
Protection Agency
Climate Protection
Partnerships Division
1200 Pennsylvania Ave. NW
Washington, DC 20460
888/782-7937 energystar.gov

National Association
of Home Builders
1201 15th St. NW
Washington, DC 20005
800/368-5242 nahb.org

National Association
of the Remodeling Industry
780 Lee St., Suite 200
Des Plaines, IL 60016
800/611-6274 nari.org

National Kitchen
and Bath Association
687 Willow Grove St.
Hackettstown, NJ 07840
800/843-6522 nkba.org

U.S. Department of Housing
and Urban Development
451 Seventh St. SW
Washington, DC 20410
202/708-1112 hud.gov

U.S. Environmental
Protection Agency
Ariel Rios Building
1200 Pennsylvania Ave. NW
Washington, DC 20460
202/343-9190 epa.gov

Contributors and Professionals

Pages 26, 65, 135, 153 (top right), 171 (bottom), 181
Field Editor: Diane Carroll
Photographer: Nancy Nolan
Bath designer: Andi Stephens,
Kitchen Distributors;
505 W. Ash St., Fayetteville, AR 72703;
479/521-1313;
kitchendistributorsinc.com

Interior designer: Andrea Cornwell,
ASID, ARID, iSpace, 1486 Woodbrook
Dr., Fayetteville, AR 72703;
479/521-7657; fax 479/521-7657;
acornwell@earthlink.net

Pages 35, 40, 49, 51 (bottom left), 156 (bottom left), 170 (bottom)
Field Editor: Diane Carroll
Photographer: Dan Piassick
Architect: Richard Drummond
Davis; 4310 Westside Dr., Suite H,
Dallas, TX 75209; 214/521-8763;
rddavisarchitect.com

Pages 113, 116, 131, 141, 148
Field Editor: Leigh Elmore
Photographer: Kim Golding
Contractor: Schloegel Design
Remodel; 311 W. 80th St., Kansas
City, MO 64114; 816/361-9669;
remodelagain.com

Pages 77, 118 (bottom right), 158, 179 (right)
Field Editor: Leigh Elmore
Photographer: Kim Golding
Contractor/Designer: Metzler
Remodeling; 3945 Main St., Suite 202,
Kansas City, MO 64111;
816/561-1453;
metzlerremodeling.com

Pages 56 (bottom), 133, 144, 155
Field Editor: Susan Andrews
Photographer: Bob Greenspan
Designer: Cindy Hedenkamp, CMH
Interiors; 6219 Valley Rd., Kansas City,
MO 64113; 816/699-3767

A designer can help guide your choice of materials. Here the choices include marble flooring and soft blue ceramic wall tiles.

GLOSSARY

Accent lighting. A beam of light three to five times brighter than general lighting that typically is used to highlight a focal point in a room.

Access panel. A removable panel in a wall or ceiling that permits repair or replacement of concealed items such as faucet bodies.

Aerator. A device screwed into the spout outlet of most sink faucets that mixes air with the water to achieve less water splash and smoother flow.

Ambient lighting. Overhead lighting that illuminates an entire room.

Backerboard. A ready-made surface for setting tile. Also called cement board.

Backsplash. Typically a 3- to 4-inch-high length of material at the back edge of a countertop extending the full length.

Batten. A narrow strip used to cover joints between boards and panels.

Beam. A horizontal support member. See also Post and Post-and-beam.

Bearing wall. An interior or exterior wall that helps support the roof or the floor joints above.

Board. A piece of lumber that is less than 2 inches thick and more than 3 inches wide.

Board foot. The standard unit of measurement for wood. One board foot is equal to a piece 12×12×1 inches (nominal size).

Building codes. Community ordinances governing the manner in which a home or other structure may be constructed or modified. Most codes deal primarily with fire and health concerns and have sections relating to electrical, plumbing, and structural work. See also Zoning.

Butt. To place materials end-to-end or end-to-edge without overlapping.

Cantilever. A beam or beams projecting beyond a support member.

Casing. Trimming around a door, window, or other opening.

Ceramic tile. Made from refined clay, usually mixed with additives and water and hardened in a kiln. Can be glazed or unglazed.

Chroma. The brightness or dullness of a hue.

Circuit. The path of electrical flow from a power source through an outlet and back to ground.

Circuit breaker. A switch that automatically interrupts electrical flow in a circuit in case of an overload or short circuit.

Codes. See Building codes.

Cornice. Any molding or group of molding used in the corner between a wall and ceiling.

Dimmer. A control that offers easy adjustment of lighting levels.

Downlight. A spotlight, either recessed or attached to the ceiling, that directs light downward.

Drain-waste-vent (DWV) system. The network of pipes and fittings that carries liquid and solid wastes out of a building to a public sewer, a septic tank, or a cesspool. It also allows for the passage of sewer gases up through the roof and to the outside.

Drapery. A decorative window treatment used to control privacy and block light.

Drywall. An interior building material consisting of sheets of gypsum that are faced with heavy paper on both sides. Also known as gypsum board or plasterboard.

Field tiles. Flat tiles with nonrounded edges used on the main portion of an installation.

Fixture. Any light or other electrical device permanently attached to a home's wiring.

Framing. The skeletal or structural support of a home, which is sometimes called framework.

General-purpose circuit. An electrical circuit that serves several light and/or receptacle outlets. See also Heavy-duty circuit.

Glazing. A protective and decorative coating, often colored, that is fired onto the surface of some tiles.

Granite. A quartz-base stone with a tough, glossy appearance; granite is harder than marble.

Ground fault circuit interrupter (GFCI). A safety device that senses any shock hazard and shuts down a circuit or receptacle.

Grout. A thin mortar mixture used to fill the joints between tiles.

Hardboard. A manufactured building material made by pressing wood fibers into sheet goods.

Hardwood. Lumber derived from deciduous trees, such as oaks, maples, and walnuts.

Header. The framing component spanning a door or window opening in a wall. A header supports the weight above it and serves as a nailing surface for the door or window frame.

Headroom. Vertical space below the ceiling that allows for standing or moving.

Heat gain. Heat coming into a home from sources other than its heating/cooling system. Most gains come from the sun.

Heat loss. Heat escaping from a home. Heat gains and losses are expressed in Btu per hour.

Heavy-duty circuit. An electrical circuit serving one 120- to 240-volt appliance. See General-purpose circuit.

Hue. Another word for color, most often used to identify a specific color.

Impervious tile. Tiles least likely to absorb water, generally used in hospitals, restaurants, and other commercial locations.

Jamb. The top and side frames of a door or window opening.

Joint compound. A synthetic-base premixed paste used in combination with paper or fiberglass tape to conceal joints between drywall panels.

Joists. Horizontal framing members that support a floor and/or ceiling.

Laminate. A hard plastic decorative veneer applied to cabinets and shelves.

Level. True horizontal. Also a tool used to determine level.

Linear foot. A term used to refer to the length of a board or piece of molding as opposed to board foot.

Lintel. A load-bearing beam over an opening, such as a door or fireplace, in masonry.

Marble. A hard and durable limestone characterized by varied patterns and colors of veins.

Molding. A strip of wood, usually small-dimensioned, used to cover exposed edges or as decoration.

Mosaic tile. Small vitreous squares or hexagons mounted on sheets or joined with adhesive strips.

Outlet. Any potential point of use in a circuit, including receptacles, switches, and light fixtures.

Panel. Wood, glass, plastic, or other material set into a frame, such as in a door. Also, a large, flat, rectangular building material such as plywood, hardboard, or drywall.

Particleboard. Panels made from compressed wood chips and glue.

Partition. An interior dividing wall that may be load-bearing.

Plywood. A material made of sheets of wood glued or cemented together.

Post. Any vertical support member.

Post-and-beam. A basic building method that uses a few hefty posts and beams to support an entire structure. Contrasts with stud framing.

Pressure-treated wood. Lumber and sheet goods impregnated with one of several solutions to make it more impervious to moisture and weather.

PVC (polyvinyl chloride). A type of plastic pipe that's suitable only for cold water.

Radiant-heat flooring. A heating system installed between the subfloor and the finished floor, using a network of electrical heating cables or tubes to hold hot water.

Receptacle. An outlet that supplies power for lamps and other plug-in devices.

Roughing in. The initial stage of a plumbing, electrical, carpentry, or other project when all components that won't be seen after the second finishing phase are assembled. Also the framing stage of a carpentry project. This framework later is concealed in the finishing stages.

Run. Any length of pipe or pipes and fittings going in a straight line.

GLOSSARY, *continued*

R-value. A measure of the resistance to heat transfer that an insulating material offers. The higher the R-value the more effective the insulation.

Sash. The part of a window that can be opened, consisting of a frame and one or more panes of glass.

Sealer. A protective, usually clear, coating applied to wood or metal.

Shower pan. The floor of a shower stall that houses the drain.

Sill. The lowest horizontal piece of a window, door, or wall framework.

Slate. A rough-surface tile split, rather than sliced, from quarried stone.

Softwood. Lumber derived from coniferous trees, such as pines, firs, cedars, or redwoods.

Stop valve. A device installed in a water supply line, usually near a fixture, that lets you shut off the water supply to one fixture without interrupting service to the rest of the system.

Stud framing. A building method that distributes structural loads to each of a series of relatively lightweight studs. Contrasts with post-and-beam.

Studs. Vertical 2×3, 2×4, or 2×6 framing members spaced at regular intervals within a wall.

Subfloor. The first layer of a floor. Usually made with planks across joists.

Task lighting. A layer of lighting targeted at specific work areas meant to illuminate and eliminate shadows.

Threshold. The plate at the bottom of some—usually exterior—door openings. Sometimes called a saddle.

Tint. The result when white is added to a color.

Tone. A color's intensity or degree of lightness or darkness.

Track lights. A versatile lighting fixture consisting of lights on a track that swivel and shift, providing general, task, or accent lighting.

Trap. The part of a fixture drain that creates a water seal to prevent sewer gases from penetrating a home's interior. Codes require that all fixtures be trapped.

Underlayment. Cementlike product that is used to level floors before laying the surface material. Sometimes used to refer to the subfloor material or material laid on top of the subfloor. Usually some type of plywood installed below the surface material of the floor. See also Subfloor.

Uniform Plumbing Code. A nationally recognized set of guidelines prescribing safe plumbing practices. Local codes take precedence when the two differ.

Universal design. The design of products or environments that allows accessibility to all people, regardless of age or ability.

Uplights. Fixtures that direct light toward the ceiling.

U-value. The amount of heat that is allowed to flow through a window.

Valance. Decorative curtain used to conceal the mounting hardware at the top of curtain fixtures.

Valve. A device to regulate the flow of water in a supply system or fixture.

Vapor barrier. A waterproof membrane in a floor, wall, or ceiling that blocks the transfer of condensation.

Veneer. A thin layer of decorative wood laminated to the surface of a more common wood.

Wainscoting. Any trim or decorative finish along the lower portion of a wall.

Water supply system. The network of pipes and fittings that transports water under pressure to fixtures and other water-using equipment and appliances.

Wet wall. A strategically placed cavity (usually a 2x6 wall) in which the main drain/vent stack and a cluster of supply and drain-waste-vent lines are housed.

Zoning. Ordinances regulating the ways in which a property may be used in a given neighborhood. Zoning laws may limit where you can locate a structure.

Sleek fixtures, gleaming mirrors, and water-hue wall tiles combine to create a serene retreat.

INDEX